About the author . . .

DAVID A. RICKS, D.B.A., is Professor of International Business, University of South Carolina. Dr. Ricks has done extensive research, as well as lectured and written about international business and marketing problems. He has testified before the U.S. House of Representatives Foreign Affairs Subcommittee on Foreign Economic Policy and has appeared on the Today Show to discuss international business problems.

Dr. Ricks has written several books, including *International Business Blunders*, and numerous articles for such publications as *The New York Times, Journal of International Business Studies, Long Range Planning, Management International Review, Journal of Advertising Research*. Articles about his work have appeared in *Business Week, Forbes*, and *The Wall Street Journal*.

Dr. Ricks received his Doctorate of Business Administration from Indiana University at which he majored in International Business Administration. He currently serves as the Treasurer of the Academy of International Business.

BIG BUSINESS BLUNDERS:

Mistakes in Multinational Marketing

DAVID A. RICKS
University of South Carolina

DOW JONES-IRWIN
Homewood, Illinois 60430

Dedicated to
all those unfortunate people
whose mistakes made this book possible

Library of Congress Catalog Card No. 82-71900
Printed in the United States of America

1 2 3 4 5 6 7 8 9 0 K 0 9 8 7 6 5 4 3

PREFACE

We often hear of business success stories. It seems that everyone is willing to relate past successes. However, unless these tales are absolutely incredible, we tend to forget them and consequently learn little of value.

Mistakes, on the other hand, are seldom admitted, are easily remembered, and can be used to illustrate valuable lessons. In fact, I began this collection of international business blunders when I discovered how effectively they could be used in the classroom. One day, after discussing what many of my students thought was a minor point related to international business, I cited a few blunders made by firms that had overlooked the concept under discussion. The students thoroughly enjoyed the blunders—so much so that not only did they remember the concepts but they wanted to learn more about international business.

As I encountered more reported blunders, I incorporated them into my classroom lectures with similar results and began to realize that I had stumbled onto a useful and enjoyable teaching tool. At this point, I decided to search seriously for blunders committed by multinational corporations. With the assistance of Professor Jeffrey S. Arpan, University of South Carolina; Marilyn Y. C. Fu Harpster, a former Ohio State University graduate student; and Professor Donald Patton, Dalhousie University, I corresponded with those teaching international business and scoured the journals and business periodicals searching for blunders. We published a few articles, and in 1974 wrote a book *International Business Blunders,* published by Grid, Inc.

The book was favorably reviewed in *Business Week* and *Forbes* and was also received well within the academic community. As I continued to gather reports of new or different blunders, the collection grew and gained the attention of the news media. As the public became aware of my collection, individuals began to send me evidence of even more blunders. All of this eventually led to suggestions that I write about those cases in multinational marketing I had uncovered.

I welcome this opportunity to share this collection with you because I truly believe that we can learn from the mistakes of others. Of course, it is not the only learning method, but it is an interesting and enjoyable one and surely preferable to learning through experience.

Many individuals have aided me in the collection and presentation of these blunders. My wife, Lesley, deserves the most credit. Not only has she been patient and supportive, but she has literally served as an editor and critic. My friends and former co-authors, Jeffrey S. Arpan, Marilyn Harpster, Donald Patton, and Vijay Mahajan, were tremendous in their encouragement and assistance in previous research efforts. I especially appreciate their understanding and tolerance of my continuing interest in these blunders. Philip Cateora was helpful in his review of the manuscript. Peter Bemelman, Kathrine Huelster, and Pedro Sanabria, graduate students in international business at the University of South Carolina, and former Ohio State University student Jeff Sugheir have also aided by serving as research assistants for this book. Dee Williams deserves credit for her efficient secretarial services. Several other people have been of assistance by sending me information about business blunders. To all these people, I wish to express my sincere appreciation.

David A. Ricks

CONTENTS

BIG BUSINESS BLUNDERS
Mistakes in Multinational Marketing

1 INTRODUCTION

International business is fraught with unexpected events. Fortunately, some of these surprising occurrences prove to be beneficial to the multinational corporations involved. For example, a U.S. firm selling feminine sanitary napkins in South America suddenly experienced a major surge in sales. The company was naturally delighted, although a bit startled when, upon investigation, it learned that the sales boost was prompted by the local farmers who were buying the napkins to use as dust masks! No less surprised was a U.S. company which sold toothbrushes in South Vietnam during the late 1960s. It also experienced a major jump in sales, but it was not until years later that the company found out the Vietcong had bought the toothbrushes not to promote white teeth but for weapon cleaning.

Other firms have also encountered unexpected markets due to unplanned and often unimagined uses for their products. These surprises, although sometimes controversial, are normally appreciated by the "lucky" corporations. However, not all companies experience such good fortune. Many surprises in international business are quite undesirable, as illustrated in the following classic examples.

A well-known multinational fiber producer purchased a large tract of land containing eucalyptus trees in Sicily. It planned to build a pulp processing plant and then use the local trees as raw material. It was not until the plant was built and production was to begin that the company discovered that the local trees were too small, the supply too limited, and the logs unsuitable for use. The result: The firm was forced to import pulp at a cost so high the plant ended up losing over $55 million dollars. This very expensive lesson occurred because the company tried to save a few dollars. To minimize costs it decided against sending a specialist to Sicily to check on the trees prior to purchase.[1]

Ill-suited or inappropriate production sites have left a deep wound in many a firm, as one U.S. food processor can attest. It built a pineapple cannery at the delta of a river in Mexico. Since the pineapple plantation was located upstream, the plan was to float the ripe fruit down to the cannery on barges. To its dismay, however, the company soon discovered that at harvest time the river current was far too strong for barge traffic. Since no other feasible alternative method of transportation existed, the plant was closed. The new equipment was sold for a fraction of its original cost to a Mexican group that immediately relocated the cannery. This seemingly simple navigational oversight proved quite expensive to the firm.[2]

A final classic example involves one of the oldest U.S. fast-food companies. This firm, having gained a great deal of domestic experience, decided to open overseas outlets. Sophisticated techniques were employed by the management, and the possible location sites were narrowed down to three addresses in Hamburg, West Germany. Careful "traffic counts" were undertaken to determine the best location, and the most frequently passed site was then purchased. A store was built, but sales were surprisingly slow. Was the traffic count in error? No! But it did turn out to be an incomplete measure. In this case, while it was true that great numbers of people were passing by the location, hamburgers were not foremost on their minds—they went by the hamburger site only because a major bordello was located next door!

These are but a few of the literally hundreds of known cases in which multinational corporations have failed to fully understand the foreign environment. Problems constantly crop up and many times cause the unexpected. Sometimes the results are unavoidable. Other times they are not. In the three cases just cited, each problem could have been foreseen and avoided.

A company is said to have "blundered" if it makes a costly or embarrassing decision even though such a result was foreseeable and avoidable. Although blunders have been made in every functional area of business, most have been experienced by companies when trying to market their products.

The task of international marketing has been far more difficult and risky than many firms expected. This is primarily due to the involvement of a great many variables—most of them uncontrollable, but recognizable. The international marketing environment is illustrated in Figure 1.

The outer and middle rings are comprised of the uncontrollable variables—foreign and domestic environmental elements, respectively. The controllable variables of the international marketing manager are in the center. No group of variables has been blunder-

FIGURE 1
The international marketing environment

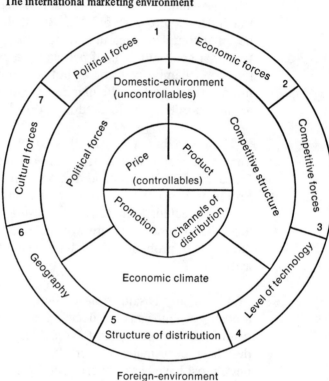

Source: Philip R. Cateora and John M. Hess, *International Marketing,* 4th ed. (Homewood, Ill.: Richard D. Irwin, 1979), p. 7.

free. In fact, blunders have resulted from a lack of concern for every single variable. It is not enough just to worry about most of the variables. Overlooking any one of them can and has caused serious problems.

The foreign environment has been especially difficult for some to analyze. Many mistakes, for example, have been made because managers have failed to recall that buyers differ from country to country. Buyers, influenced by local economic constraints and by local values, attitudes, and tastes, differ in what they buy, why they buy, how they buy, when they buy, where they buy, and who makes the purchasing decisions. Managers who have failed to recognize these differences have committed a number of blunders. In fact, "it is the international differences in buyer behavior, rather than the similarities, which pose stumbling blocks to successful international marketing. Thus the differences must receive disproportionate attention from the marketer."[3]

THE ROLE OF CULTURE

'Cultural differences are the most significant and troublesome variables for the multinational company.' The failure of managers to comprehend fully these disparities has led to most international business blunders. A European businessman, for example, while on an important negotiating trip to China, playfully flipped a piece of ice from his drink at his companion. Unluckily for him, the ice accidentally landed on a nearby official, so he was soon sent packing. Another unlucky individual found himself home sooner than expected after he flippantly patted a waitress. The Chinese simply do not accept such foolishness— as many a playful visitor has discovered.

'All nationalities possess unique characteristics that must be understood.' For example, the Arabs dislike deadlines.'An Arab faced with a deadline tends to feel threatened and backed into a corner. Many Americans, on the other hand, often try to expedite matters by setting deadlines. Hundreds of American-owned radio sets are therefore sitting untouched in Middle Eastern repair shops because Americans made the cultural error of asking for the work to be completed by a certain time.

American managers have encountered similar problems trying to understand time values in other cultures as well. One U.S. company lost a major contract opportunity in Greece because its managers tried to impose American customs on the Greek negotiators. Besides being too forthright and outspoken in the eyes of the Greeks, the Americans endeavored to set time limits for the meetings. The Greeks, however, considered time limits insulting and felt they showed a lack of finesse. The Americans also wanted the Greeks to first agree to principles and then have subordinates work out the necessary details. The Greeks viewed this as a deceptive U.S. strategy since they prefer to work out everything—regardless of the time it takes.[4]

Sometimes the failure to understand cultural differences can have even more serious consequences. As an example, consider the unfortunate American manager working in the South Pacific. He had foolishly hired local natives without regard to the traditional status system of the island. By hiring too many of one group, he threatened to change the balance of power and traditions of the people. The islanders talked over this unacceptable situation and independently came up with an alternative plan. But it had taken them until 3 a.m. to do so. Since time was not important in their culture, they saw no reason to wait until morning to make their suggestions known to the American. They casually went to his place of residence, but their arrival at such a late hour caused him to panic. Since he could not understand their language and could not imagine that they would want to talk business at 3 a.m., he assumed that they were

coming to riot—or worse, so he called in the marines!
It was some time before the company was able to get
back to "business as usual."

To be effective in a foreign environment, it is usually necessary to understand the local culture. Knowing what to do is as important as knowing what not
to do. In India, for instance, it is considered a viola-
tion of sacred hospitality mores to discuss business in
the home or on social occasions. At the same time, if
a businessman from India offers "come any time," he
means it. In the United States this may simply be a
polite expression, but in India it represents a serious
invitation. The Indian is requesting a visit but is politely allowing the guest to arrange the time of the
meeting. If no time is set, the Indian assumes the invitation has been refused. Failure to understand this
local custom has led to serious misunderstandings between business people.

Even the rejection of a cup of coffee can cause major problems. While a very profitable opportunity was
being negotiated, one U.S. executive innocently made
the mistake of turning down a Saudi Arabian businessman's friendly offer to join him for a cup of coffee. The American was in a hurry to close the deal,
but such a rejection is considered an affront there.
Naturally, the Saudi became much less sociable, and
the negotiation process was much less successful than
it would have been.

Gift-giving can also create problems. Sometimes
gifts are expected, and the failure to supply them
proves insulting. Other times, however, the mere offer
of such a token is considered offensive. In the Middle
East, for example, hosts are insulted if guests bring
food or drink to their homes because it implies that

they are not good hosts. (Liquor, of course, is an especially dangerous gift as it is prohibited by the Islamic religion.) 'In many parts of Latin America, cutlery or handkerchiefs should not be given because these gifts imply a cutting off of a relationship or the likelihood of a tearful event. And giving a clock to someone in China is not a good idea, either. The Chinese word for clock sounds the same as their word for funeral.'

'In fact, even the way in which a gift is presented is important. In most parts of Asia gifts should be given privately to avoid embarrassing the Asians, but they need to be offered publicly in the Middle East to reduce the possible impression that bribery is being attempted.[5]'

To avoid making blunders, a person must be able to discern the difference between what must be done (a "cultural imperative"), what must not be done (a "cultural exclusive"), and what may or may not be done (a "cultural adiaphora"). Shoes must be removed before entering many of the world's religious buildings, but the individuals doing so must not act as if they are of the religion if, in fact, they are not.

Complete knowledge and understanding of a foreign culture, however, is almost impossible to acquire. In fact, no general agreement even exists as to what "culture" is, but most do agree that it is a complex set of variables involving a group's beliefs and ways of living. In a classic article on the subject of culture and its effect upon business, Edward T. Hall emphasizes time, space, material possessions, friendship patterns, and forms of agreement as basic components.[6] A noted anthropologist groups the elements as material culture, social institutions, belief systems, aesthetics, and language.[7] A pair of well-known researchers of comparative management group 29 cultural characteristics into 4 sets: educational, sociological, political-legal, and economic.[8] And in his book on the cultural environment of international business, Vern Terpstra illustrates the complexity of culture in a diagram shown here in Figure 2.[9]

Although these scholars do not agree on the best grouping of the variables, the lists and classifications clearly indicate that culture is indeed complex and an understanding of any foreign culture requires knowledge in a great many areas. Unfortunately, even a well-intended person can make a blunder by overlooking just one seemingly unimportant aspect of a foreign culture. As in Figure 1, oversights in each of the categories listed in Figure 2 have led to errors. All of the areas need to be scrutinized.

THE ROLE OF COMMUNICATION

As stated, culture plays an important part in the drama of multinational marketing. Of all of the aspects of culture, communication may be the most critical and certainly has been involved in a number of blunders. Good communication linkages must be established between a company and its customers, its suppliers, its employees, and the governments of the countries where it performs business activities. Poor communication networks between any of these areas can, and have, caused difficulties.

One source of trouble especially trying to companies is that of effective communication with potential buyers. The problem is that there are many potential communication barriers. The most troublesome are

FIGURE 2
The cultural environment of international business

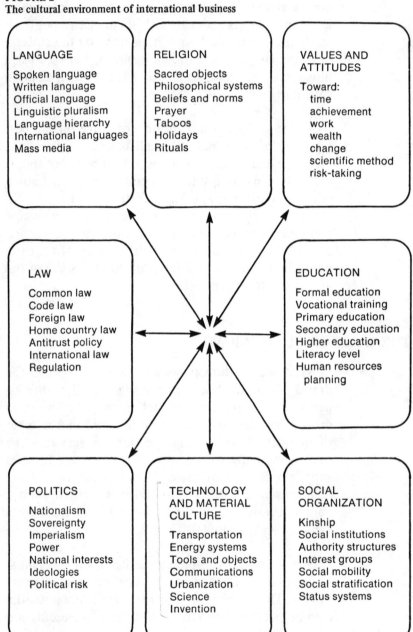

Source: Vern Terpstra, *Cultural Environment of International Business* (Cincinnati: South-Western Publishing, 1978), p. xiv.

shown in Figure 3. Messages can be translated incorrectly, inappropriate media used, regulations overlooked, and economic or taste differences ignored. Sometimes the intended buyer does not receive the message. Other times the message arrives but due to its ineffectiveness is of no value. Once in a while the buyer receives the message, but to the company's dismay, the message sent was incorrect. Multinational corporations both send and receive information. Incorrect actions occurring in either direction have been responsible for blunders.

FIGURE 3
Communication barriers in international marketing

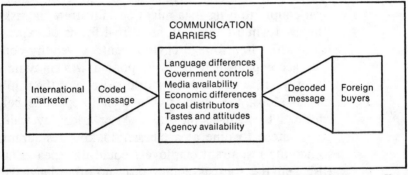

Source: From Vern Terpstra, *International Dimensions of Marketing* (Boston: Kent Publishing Company, 1981), p. 158. © 1981 by Wadsworth, Inc. Reprinted by permission of Kent Publishing Company, a division of Wadsworth, Inc., 20 Park Plaza, Boston, MA 02116.

Multinational corporations are not the only entities vulnerable to communication problems, of course. Former President Carter's speech in Poland will long be remembered for his incorrectly translated appreciation of the Polish women (whom his translator said he "lusted for"). Former President Kennedy, in a major speech in Berlin, tried to say he was proud to be from Berlin but actually remarked that he was proud to be a jelly-filled donut (a "Berliner")./Other well-known people have mangled public introductions terribly by using incorrect titles and names. It seems that if there is a way to say something incorrectly, some poor soul has managed to do so.

Communication problems are not necessarily verbal. Nonverbal communication difficulties have also led to serious blunders.

Nonverbal communication exists in many forms. Some kinds are intended to supplement verbal communication; others are used when verbal communication is not possible. A true anecdote about an American couple touring Asia might best illustrate the risks involved when relying on nonverbal forms of expression while in a foreign environment. A wealthy couple, accompanied by their pet poodle, was enjoying a lengthy cruise around the world. At one of the ship's Asian stops, the couple, with their inseparable pet, decided to sightsee the town. After a lengthy walk, they chose to dine at a pleasant-looking restaurant. Since the restaurant employees could not speak English and the tourists could speak no other language, they ordered their meals by pointing to various items on the menu. Knowing that the poodle was also hungry, the couple tried to order food for it. For a long time the waiter had a difficult time understanding, but after several attempts he seemed to have figured it all out. He pointed to the dog and then pointed to the kitchen. The couple interpreted this to mean that their pet could not eat in the dining area but must eat in the kitchen where the waiter had some food for it. They therefore agreed to let the waiter take the dog to the kitchen. After waiting a particularly long time, the waiter and the full staff proudly entered with the couple's order. One can imagine the tourists' horror when the chef lifted one of the lids to display how well he had cooked the poodle!

There are many forms of nonverbal communication. Some of the most important are:

Appearances
Chronemics
Haptics
Kinesics
Oculesics
Olfactions
Orientations
Paralinguistics
Postures
Proxemics

Appearances include physical attire and grooming. Sometimes an individual's appearance can convey a stronger or a different message than is intended. Each culture holds different expectations and norms. Sloppy attire, for example, can prove more offensive in some countries than in others. Chronemics is the timing of verbal exchanges. Americans, for example, tend to expect prompt responses whereas others sometimes prefer much slower response times. Haptics is the use of touch while conversing and is generally used much less by Americans than by people of other nationalities. Kinesics is the movement of part of the body to communicate. In some cultures, a great deal of hand movement is normal. Hands, however, are used much less by Americans than by the French or Italians. Oculesics is the use (or avoidance) of eye contact for communication and is utilized by

Americans more often than by peoples of many other cultures./ Olfaction is the action of smelling./ Some cultures deliberately use specific odors to convey messages, but the smells and their interpretations vary from country to country./ Orientations are the angles at which people position themselves in relation to each other./ A face-to-face position can convey friendship in one country but confrontation in another. /Paralinguistics are the nonverbal aspects of speech./ /They include emotional tones, accents, and the quality of the voice./ A nervous person often speaks quickly whereas an angry individual is likely to speak more slowly and more loudly. Postures, the many different bodily positions of standing, sitting, lying, and so on, generally convey interpersonal attitudes which are culturally defined. Certain postures represent friendly, antagonistic, superior, or other attitudes. Proxemics is the use of space in communication. South Americans, Greeks, and Japanese feel more comfortable standing or sitting closer to strangers than do members of many other nationalities.[10]

Misunderstandings and blunders have resulted from the misinterpretation of all of these nonverbal means of communication. The old proverb, for instance, that "patience is a virtue" is all too often forgotten by Americans. On many occasions, this lapse of memory has led them to react inappropriately by trying to correct a situation when in actuality all that was required was patience. The "improper" amount of touching or eye contact has left many people feeling so uncomfortable that effective communication efforts have been hampered. The "incorrect" distance between individuals engaged in conversation has led to the false conclusion that the other person is too aggressive and hostile or too cold and distrustful.

The peoples of each culture uniquely utilize body movements as methods of communication. The meanings of motions and signs common in one culture may relay something quite different in another. Consider, for example, the OK sign commonly used in the United States. In France it signifies zero, and in Japan it is a symbol for money. In parts of South America, however, it is a vulgar gesture. At least one company has learned this expensive lesson. It had an entire catalog printed with the OK stamp on each page. Although the error was quickly discovered, it created a costly six-month delay while all of the catalogs were reprinted.

Head shakes are particularly difficult to interpret. People in the United States shake their heads up and down to signify "yes." Many British, however, make the same motions just to indicate that they hear—not necessarily that they agree. To say "no," people shake their heads from side to side in the United States, jerk their heads back in a haughty manner in the Middle East, wave a hand in front of the face in the Orient, and shake a finger from side to side in Ethiopia.

Asian Indians sometimes shift their heads in a slightly jerky manner from side to side to indicate interest. In New Zealand, people suck in a bit of air to show that same interest. The U.S. gesture to slit one's throat means "I love you" in Swaziland. The backward victory symbol is an insulting gesture in Europe. The use of a palm-up hand and moving index finger connotes "come here" in many countries but is vulgar in others. In Ethiopia, one beckons by holding out the hand, palm down, and repeatedly closing the hand. The act of folding one's arms denotes respect in Fiji but indicates arrogance in Finland. One finger to the lips to an Ethiopian requests silence from a child whereas four fingers to the lips are necessary to ask the same from an adult.

The pointing of a finger is a dangerous action. In North America it is a very normal gesture, but it is considered very rude in many other parts of the world—especially in areas of Asia and Africa. It is therefore much safer to merely close the hand and point with the thumb.

Many cultures also have their own form of greeting. Often it is some variation of a handshake, but people greet each other with hugs, nose rubs, kisses, and other gestures in other cultures. Failure to be aware of these customs has led to awkward and embarrassing encounters and to serious misunderstandings.

Other forms of communication have also caused problems. The tone of the voice, for example, can be important. Some cultures permit people to raise their voices when they are not close to each other, but loudness in other cultures is often associated with anger or a loss of self-control.

Even laughter is interpreted differently around the world. While most countries consider it an expression of joy, some cultures discourage it. In many West African countries, laughter indicates embarrassment, discomfort, or surprise.

A lack of knowledge of such differences in verbal and nonverbal forms of communication has resulted in many a social and corporate blunder. Local people tend to be willing to overlook most of the mistakes of tourists; after all, they are just temporary visitors.

Locals are much less tolerant of the errors of business people—especially those who represent firms trying to project an impression of permanent interest in the local economy. The consequences of erring, therefore, are much greater for the corporation.

STRUCTURE

Some of the big business blunders that corporations have made while marketing their products in foreign countries are described and discussed in this book. Most of these blunders have been reported in the media, but only in small numbers at any one time and in no clear patterns. The gathering of hundreds of these reports provided an opportunity to group these marketing blunders and to arrive at some universally applicable conclusions.

The blunders have been grouped into six categories: adaptation, name, promotion, translation, strategy, and market research. The problems encountered by multinational corporations when they have failed to adequately adapt products or packages are discussed in Chapter 2. This chapter also cites examples of incorrect modifications.

As pointed out in Chapter 3, names can also cause corporate headaches. Inappropriate product and company names have been involved in costly decisions. On occasion, the blunder has been the company's introduction of an old, established name in a country which misunderstands it. In other instances, the company created a new name, only to later regret it. Sometimes harmless and amusing, these blunders have at other times proven insulting, embarrassing, and costly.

Promotional mistakes are described in Chapter 4. Communication problems, improper personnel, incorrect strategies, legal oversights, and cultural differences have all played a part in the development of major promotional blunders in overseas markets. These types of errors are identified and discussed.

The largest number of promotional blunders has been due to faulty translations. In fact, the number of translation errors is so vast that they are reported in a separate chapter, Chapter 5. Carelessness, unexpected additional meanings, and improper use of idioms have all contributed to translation blunders. Lessons can be gleaned from these mistakes, including the value of using local people, using "backtranslation," developing proper selection methods for translators, and determining what can be done to aid the translator. These guidelines are presented in Chapter 5 along with the conclusion that, in some instances, it just might be better not to translate.

Errors in marketing strategy are cited in Chapter 6. Some of the mistakes are based on supply or logistical problems; others have involved the improper selection of overseas partners. Pricing strategies have been the downfall of some firms, but for others the problems encountered were much more complex. Even though mistakes in strategy have caused some of the most costly blunders, one should realize that they are among the most difficult to avoid. No easy solutions are given, but some of the methods which might reduce the number of strategic errors are noted.

In Chapter 7, feasibility studies, market research, and the possibility of "no market" are discussed. The necessity of proper research is stressed and illustrated.

Concluding comments and observations are found in the Epilogue. Many of these comments relate to the interpretability of the findings. Among other things, please note that this book is not intended to poke fun at corporations. Neither does it make it possible for someone to conclude that firms are constantly making foolish mistakes. The overall record is good, but hopefully this book will help make the future record even better.

2 ADAPTATION

In the United States, we tend to take for granted the vast array of products available for sale. In other countries, however, such product variety and selection does not always exist. The assumption that the absence of a product from another economy automatically indicates a potentially good or profitable market has led a number of companies down a thorny path. More than one company has failed to consider that even if the local consumers can afford the product, they may not really want it or may be interested in it only if it is substantially modified to fit their local tastes and preferences.

These modifications, known as adaptations, exist in two major forms: product and package. Product modification or the alteration of the physical product is occasionally required for the product to conform to local tastes or local conditions. Adaptation of the package is often necessary to attract the customer to the product or to maintain the product's integrity in a unique environment. Occasionally, a firm is forced to modify both the package and the product to create a suitable product for the new market.

PRODUCT

The Campbell Soup Company discovered that product modification can be a simpler road to travel than consumer education when it tried to market its condensed soups in Great Britain. The company had used market testing methods to confirm a British interest in its soups and had also priced the soup to be competitive. But initial sales were low, a result of the failure of the British to understand that, in fact, the Campbell's soup was priced competitively. The British were accustomed to buying canned soup but not in the condensed form. Therefore, it appeared to them that they were buying half as much soup for the same amount of money. Campbell Soup was faced with two choices. It could try to hurriedly mass educate the British buying public or it could alter the product. It wisely chose to modify its product by adding water in order for it to be like the soups already accepted and found on the grocery shelves.[1]

General Foods experienced similar difficulties when it tried to sell its American-style Jell-O in Great Britain. Although the package of Jell-O contained the normal powdered substance Americans expect when buying Jell-O, the British simply were not interested. In Great Britain, the jelled form of such a product is the normal one to buy. To a Briton, if it does not jiggle and look good, then it simply isn't "proper." By quickly changing its product to conform to the British norm, General Foods averted a possible disaster.[2]

The sale of cigarettes outside the home country has been quite exasperating for several companies. The common presumption that all peoples enjoy identical products has often proven erroneous; in fact, some form of product modification has usually been necessary to gain market success. The failure to make the needed alteration, even though possibly a slight one, can radically hurt sales. More than one firm, for example, has encountered difficulties trying to sell filter-tipped cigarettes in the less-developed countries. Consumers of the wealthier nations are more aware of the health risks, so they are quite willing to pay a bit more for the filtered cigarettes. In poor countries, where life expectancy is often less than 30 years, the threat of death from lung cancer is lessened. Even if aware of the risks, the local smoker can usually neither afford the extra cost of the filtered cigarettes nor become too concerned about developing lung cancer at an advanced age. Consequently, the market for filtered cigarettes in these countries is typically sluggish. Often the only modification needed to increase sales is the removal of the filter and the accompanying reduction in price.[3]

Some products may require more technical modification. Obviously, if the electrical current available in the potential market is different, then electrical products require adaptation before introduction. Measurement systems vary between countries, and often components need to be modified to adhere to local standards. Product sizes must be considered. A British firm, for example, experienced problems selling in Japan until it remodeled its product $\frac{1}{16}$th of an inch to conform to Japanese specifications. Such small differences can easily cause major headaches for manufacturers. Fortunately, most companies quickly learn of these local standards and conditions and seldom introduce a totally inappropriate product. A much more difficult task is the detection of the subtle technical differences and the needed modifications.

A duplicating machine manufacturer ran into serious problems in one country when it assumed the availability of the quality paper required for use in its machines. In this case, the local government owned its own paper company. Unfortunately, the paper size and quality were not highly standardized, and the imported machines could not accommodate the varying characteristics. Due to the government's pride in its paper facilities, however, it would not allow the importation of the paper required. The machines sat idle, and the company's market was quickly closed. The company should have learned of this problem prior to its market entry. It then could have requested permission to import the correct paper, or it could have modified its machines to accommodate the local paper. Had neither been possible, the firm would have known not to market its products in that country.

Refrigerator manufacturers from the Western nations initially encountered great difficulty in selling their products in Japan. The refrigerator motors presented the major problem; they were simply too noisy for the typical Japanese home which was often built with literally paper-thin walls. Sears is cited as one of the companies most successful in the sale of western refrigerators in Japan. It achieved this status by designing a refrigerator specifically for use in the local conditions.

General Motors of Canada experienced major technical problems in Iraq. It shipped 13,500 Chevrolet Malibu automobiles there only to discover that the cars were mechanically unfit for the hot and dusty climate. Iraq would not even accept delivery of the remaining 12,000 autos which had been ordered until GM modified the vehicles so that they would work reliably. GM tripled its number of engineers and mechanics in Baghdad, but by the time the company figured out that supplementary air filters and different clutches would eliminate the mechanical failures, it began to encounter political problems. At last report, 12,000 automobiles specially designed for desert driving were collecting snow in Canada.[4]

Unexpected major adjustments also had to be made by an American tire producer after it opened a plant in France. Based on its previous success in France, the tire manufacturer built a new production facility without market research. Due to the changing driving habits of the French, however, new kinds of tires were necessary and adjustments were forced upon the manufacturer. The company learned its lesson, of course. It hired a market research executive before building its next plant.

The necessity for product adaptation has existed for hundreds of years. England's East India Company possibly lost control of India in 1857 because it failed to modify a product it provided. In those days bullets were often encased in pig wax, and the tops had to be bitten off before the bullets could be fired. The Asian Indian soldiers were furious when they discovered the pig wax since it was against their religion to eat pork. The soldiers revolted and hundreds were killed on both sides before peace was restored. The bullets were modified, but the East India Company lost control of India to the British Crown.[5]

Taste

One variable often requiring modification is taste. Both the food and tobacco industries can attest to this. Philip Morris encountered well-publicized problems when it tried to sell its U.S. blends in Canada. Many other companies have experienced similar difficulties in other countries. Most cigarette firms believe that "it is better to switch than fight," and cigarettes are now generally blended in deference to local taste preferences.

Vast numbers of food products have required taste adaptations in order to appeal to local consumers. General Foods experienced such problems and had to alter some of its coffees and foods to attract European and Japanese palates. Campbell Soup Company also was forced to change the flavor of some of its soups (notably the tomato soup) to suit European preferences. Many soft drinks have been modified to gain market acceptance in various parts of the world. Often all that is necessary is a subtle change, but without such variation, sales may slump. Both General Foods and Campbell Soup Company have enjoyed overseas successes because they realized this and acted accordingly. Nestle's has also successfully introduced dozens of blends of its Nescafé around the world. Kentucky Fried Chicken initiated one of the more unique product modifications. In order to sell its chicken in Israel, it introduced a modified product—Kosher chicken.[6]

U.S. companies are not the only ones that have found local tastes different from those at home. European soups, for example, are considered too salty by most Americans and have not fared well on U.S. grocery shelves.

Food and tobacco manufacturers have not borne the effects of consumer preference alone. Style is another important ingredient in the product mix, and failure to reflect local style choices is also likely to cause financial losses for a company. Ford experienced well-publicized problems in Europe during the

1960s partially as a result of the amount of "Americanization" being introduced into the look of its European cars. Earlier style lines of Ford's European cars sold well in Europe because of their simple sleekness which was favored by the local people. When the more traditional aspects of the American automobile (i.e., wideness, heaviness, length) were incorporated into models of the 1960s, sales slumped. The sales resistance came to a halt when the cars produced once again reflected European tastes.[7]

Cluett, Peabody may have had similar problems as its Belgian factory was closed after only three years. Cluett blames high costs for the closing; but Belgian retailers claim it was really due to a complaisant Belgian management which assented to American styling, pricing, and sizing that were not in harmony with European tastes and budgets. Either cause for failure could have been eliminated through appropriate preliminary research and implementation of the indicated modifications.

From the above examples, it should be clear that environmental factors influence many product designs. Several of the environmental factors that may force product adaptation are listed in the left column of Table 2-1. The corresponding type of necessary product change is reported in the right column.

PACKAGE

In many markets, the product may be quite acceptable but still may not sell well if housed in an inappropriate package. Packages play two key roles in marketing—they promote the product and they protect it. Packages that require long-distance shipping must be capable of withstanding the journey. Many companies have endeavored to export their products only to witness the return of crushed and partially empty containers. Others have tried to ship perishable goods via means requiring months for delivery. Still others have placed the goods in packages unable to withstand moisture (or other unique conditions). In some climates, packages must be specially designed to assure product survival. Quaker Oats, for example, uses special vacuum-sealed tins to protect its products sold in hot and humid countries.

Local storage conditions also vary, and the package must be an appropriate size and shape. Coca-Cola

TABLE 2-1
Design implications of environmental factors

Environmental factors	Product design implications
Level of technical skills	Product simplification
Level of labor cost	Automation or manualization of the product
Level of literacy	Remarking and simplification of the product
Level of income	Quality and price change
Level of interest rates	Quality and price-change (Investment in quality might not be financially desirable.)
Level of maintenance	Change in tolerances
Climatic differences	Product adaptation
Isolation (heavy repair difficult and expensive)	Product simplification and reliability improvement
Differences in standards	Recalibration of product and resizing
Availability of other products	Greater or lesser product integration
Availability of materials	Change in product structure and fuel
Power availability	Resizing of product
Special conditions	Product redesign or invention

Source: Richard D. Robinson, "The Challenge of the Underdeveloped National Market," *Journal of Marketing,* Vol. 25, October 1961, p. 22. Published by the American Marketing Association.

tried to introduce the two-liter plastic bottle in Spain, but market entry was difficult. The company soon discovered that few Spaniards had refrigerator doors with compartments large enough to accommodate that size bottle.

Containers occasionally embarrass a company. U.S.-made medical containers drew a great deal of unwanted attention when they were used in Great Britain. The containers carried the instructions: "Take off top and push in bottom." This message, considered harmless in the United States, bore very sexual and humorous connotations to the British. Needless to say, the containers were soon modified.

Seemingly harmless package labels have sometimes proven to be embarrassing to the company or even insulting to the potential consumers. One soft-drink company inadvertently offended some of its customers in the Arab world because its labels incorporated six-pointed stars. The stars were only considered to be a decoration by the firm, but they were interpreted by the Arabs as reflecting pro-Israeli sentiments. Naturally, the label had to be altered.

In areas where many of the people are illiterate, the label usually depicts a picture of what the package contains. This very logical practice proved to be quite perplexing to one big company. It tried to sell baby food in an African nation by using its regular label showing a baby and stating the type of baby food in the jar. Unfortunately, the local population took one look at the labels and interpreted them to mean the jars contained ground-up babies! Sales, of course, were terrible.

Some European dry soup producers have solved

their marketing problems in the United States by altering their labels. Rather than trying to change the product, they merely developed different uses for the product and stated this on the package label. American and European dried soups are packaged identically but labeled differently. The U.S. package emphasizes the use of the product as a sauce or dip. As expected, U.S. sales were much better once the firm stressed the nonsoup use.

Even something as innocuous as a wrapping can cause trouble. A New York exporter agreed to send some products to an Arab country and thoughtlessly wrapped the goods in local newspapers for shipment. The customer was arrested and his goods confiscated when the Arab customs inspectors opened up the packages and found that the wrappings used were Jewish newspapers.

The use of numbers provides another source of blundering. Each country has its own special lucky and unlucky numbers, and using the wrong number can indeed be unlucky. A U.S. golf-ball manufacturer, for example, tried to sell golf balls to the Japanese packaged in groups of four. Problems arose because the pronunciation of the word *four* in Japanese also sounds like the Japanese word for *death.* The number four, therefore, is considered undesirable, and items grouped into fours simply don't sell well.

Color

The choice of package and product coloring is very tricky. Sometimes companies have failed to sell their products overseas and have never known why. Often the reason was a simple one; the product or its container was merely an inappropriate color.

For instance, green, a popular color in many Moslem countries, is often associated with disease in countries with dense, green jungles. It is associated with cosmetics by the French, Dutch, and Swedes. Various colors represent death. Black signifies death to Americans and many Europeans, but in Japan and many other Asian countries, white represents death. (Obviously white wedding gowns are not popular with numbers of Asians.) Latin Americans generally associate purple with death, but dark red is the appropriate mourning color along the Ivory Coast. And even though white is the color representing death to some, it expresses joy to those living in Ghana. In many countries, bright colors such as yellow and orange express joy. To most of the world, blue is thought to be a masculine color, but it is not as manly as red in the United Kingdom or France. In Iran, blue represents a bad color. Although pink is believed to be the foremost feminine color by Americans, most of the rest of the world considers yellow to be the most feminine color. Red is felt to be blasphemous in some African countries but is generally considered to be a color reflecting wealth or luxury elsewhere. A red circle has been successfully used on many packages sold in Latin America, but it is unpopular in some parts of Asia. To them it conjures up images of the Japanese flag.

Pictures of flowers can be found on many package labels, but there, too, caution is required. Certain flowers and their colors can convey hidden messages. In France and many countries which have experienced a British influence, the white lily is often used for funerals. Mexicans, though, use lilies to lift superstitious spells. A purple flower symbolizes death to a Brazilian, but yellow flowers represent death or disrespect in Mexico. In France and the Soviet Union, however, the yellow flower signifies infidelity.

Legal

Because most countries maintain regulations concerning their products and packages, it may be the wording on the package or label rather than a "bad" color that creates difficulties. Countries expect foreign marketers to adhere to rules, and failure to do so may prove costly. Coca-Cola, for instance, aroused the anger of the Italians when it printed the mandatory list of ingredients on the bottle cap. Local courts ruled that the cap was easily tossed away and, therefore, did not serve as an acceptable location for this list. Coca-Cola, of course, quickly modified its package and listed the ingredients on the bottles themselves, but the incident was not without its costs.

In Australia, the manufacturer of Aim toothpaste was taken to court by one of its competitors because of an Australian law that prohibits the sale of competitive products in similar packages. A very strict interpretation and enforcement of this law forced Unilever to change its Aim package even though it had spent $5 million on Aim's promotion. The error was costly, but it was correctable with the appropriate alterations.[8]

SUMMARY

Product and package modifications are often required to enhance a product's appeal to the foreign consumer. Sometimes the alterations are minor; other times they are more complex. Market testing can help a firm avoid the entry of an inappropriate product, but the failure to initiate such studies or develop thorough ones has led a number of companies to blunder.

In all fairness to multinational firms, however, market tests can be quite tricky to initiate and conduct. It is difficult indeed to "cover all the angles," and one of the hardest tasks is the identification of the proper testing locations. Since firms cannot always afford to test each product everywhere, sample areas are normally identified as being representative of a country or region. Some companies have used an area of France for their West European test market. Others have used Belgium. Each firm must determine the region most appropriate for its product. This is no easy task. In fact, a combination of locations may be necessary. Wherever these places are, though, they must be found, because market testing is essential.

3   NAMES

Shakespeare once queried, "What's in a name?" A number of business people, after a bit of international marketing, might appropriately respond, "More than you might think." Many companies have discovered that even something as seemingly innocuous as a name can prove insulting and embarrassing. Both product and company names can fall prey to such troubles.

PRODUCT NAMES

Product names often take on various unintended and hidden meanings. The experience of a major soapmaker serves as a classic example. When this company was considering a name for a new soap powder to be marketed internationally, it wisely ran a translation test of the proposed soap name in 50 major languages. In English and most of the major European languages, the name meant "dainty." In other tongues, however, the soap name did not translate so appropriately. In Gaelic, it became "song," in Flemish it meant "aloof," and it said "horse" in the language of one African tribe. In Persia, the name was translated as "hazy" or "dimwitted," and to the Koreans, the name sounded like a person out of his mind. Finally, in all of the Slavic languages, the name was considered obscene and offensive. Naturally, the proposed name was hastily abandoned. This experience, though, demonstrates the importance of a name and how carefully it should be considered prior to the introduction of the product.

Unusual problems

Today, more and more firms are seeking assistance in hopes of avoiding costly and embarrassing mistakes. Even the largest and most sophisticated firms are not immune to the difficulties of product-name interpretation. For example, when the Coca-Cola Company was planning its strategy for marketing in China in the 1920s, it wanted to introduce its product with the English pronunciation of "Coca-Cola." A translator developed a group of Chinese characters which, when pronounced, sounded like the product name. These characters were placed on the cola bottles and marketed. Was it any wonder that sales levels were low? The characters actually translated to mean "a wax-flattened mare" or "bite the wax tadpole." Since the product was new, sound was unimportant to the consumers; meaning was vital.[1] Today Coca-Cola is again marketing its cola in China. The new characters used on the bottle translate to "happiness in the mouth." From its first marketing attempts, Coca-Cola learned a valuable lesson in international marketing.

General Motors was faced with a similar problem. It was troubled by the lack of enthusiasm among the Puerto Rican auto dealers for its recently introduced Chevrolet "Nova." The name "Nova" meant "star" when literally translated. However, when spoken, it sounded like "no va" which, in Spanish, means "it doesn't go." This obviously did little to increase consumer confidence in the new vehicle. To remedy the situation, General Motors changed the automobile name to "Caribe" and sales increased.

Other car manufacturers have also experienced comparable situations. In fact, problems with the names used in international automobile promotions seem to be frequent events. For example, difficulties arose during the translation of the name of the American car "Randan." Apparently this name was interpreted by the Japanese to mean "idiot." The American Motors Corporation's "Matador" name usually conjures up images of virility and strength, but in Puerto Rico it means "killer"–not a favorable connotation in a place with a high traffic fatality rate.

Ford encountered translation problems with some of its cars as well. It introduced a low cost truck, the "Fiera," into some of the less-developed countries. Unfortunately the name meant "ugly old woman" in Spanish. Needless to say, this name did not encourage sales. Ford also experienced slow sales when it introduced a top-of-the-line automobile, the "Comet," in Mexico under the name "Caliente." The puzzlingly low sales levels were finally understood when Ford discovered that "caliente" is slang for a streetwalker. Additional headaches were reportedly experienced when Ford's "Pinto" was briefly introduced in Brazil under its English name. The name was speedily changed to "Corcel" (which means "horse" in Portuguese) after Ford discovered that the Portuguese slang translation of "pinto" is "a small male appendage."

The naming of a new automobile model to be marketed in Germany by Rolls Royce was a difficult undertaking. The company felt that the English name "Silver Mist" was very appealing but discovered that the name would undoubtedly not capture the German market as hoped. In German, the translated meaning of "mist" is actually "excrement," and the Germans could not possibly have found such a name appealing. Unfortunately, the Sunbeam Corporation did not learn of this particular translation problem in time and attempted to enter the German market advertising its new mist-producing hair curling iron, the "Mist-Stick." As should have been expected, the Germans had no interest in a "dung" or "manure" wand.

Firms occasionally try to enter the foreign market promoting a product bearing an untranslated name. Sometimes this tactic works, but other times it does not work as well as expected. At least one global firm can attest to this. The company consistently marketed one of its pieces of equipment under the name "Grab Bucket." To its chagrin, the firm learned that in Germany it was actually advertising the sale of cemetery plot flowers. In German, the word *grab* is interpreted as *grave,* and *bucket* is pronounced like *bouquet.* So because of these linguistic anomalies, the company did not appear to be selling what it thought at all.

Many companies have suffered similar pitfalls. A U.S. company was taken by surprise when it introduced its product in Latin America and learned that the name of the product meant "jackass oil" in Spanish. Another well-intentioned firm sold shampoo in Brazil under the name "Evitol." Little did it realize that it was claiming to be selling a "dandruff contraceptive." A manufacturing company sold its machines in the Soviet Union under the name "Bardak"—a word which signifies a brothel in Russian. An American product failed to capture the Swedish market; the product name translated to "enema," which the product was not. A Finnish brewery introduced two new beverages in the United States—"Koff" beer and "Siff" beer. Is it any wonder that sales were sluggish? Another name, unappealing to Americans, can be found on the package of a delicious chocolate and fruit product sold in the German or European deli. The chocolate concoction has the undesirable English name "Zit!"

The reported troubles of an American company that markets Pet milk serves as one more example. This firm reportedly experienced difficulties introducing its product in French-speaking areas. It seems that the word *Pet* in French means, among other things, "to break wind." And had Colgate-Palmolive attempted to gain market entry with its Cue toothpaste in French-speaking regions, it too would have encountered comparable problems. *Cue* is a pornographic word in French.[2] An American woman will long remember her international experience with Coca-Cola. She was dispensing sample tasters of Fresca soda pop when she unintentionally elicited a great deal of laughter from passersby. She only later realized the cause when she discovered that in Mexican slang the word *Fresca* means *lesbian.*

Close examination of foreign markets and language differences are necessary and should be required before a product's domestically successful name is introduced abroad. Unfortunately, this simple warning is sometimes neglected in a company's enthusiasm to plunge into overseas marketing operations.

Manufacturers often assume that products which have enjoyed domestic success will naturally receive the same reception overseas. However, this is not always the case as the following examples demonstrate. Princess Housewares, Inc., a large U.S. appliance

manufacturer, introduced a line of electric housewares in the German market. The company's brand
name, well known and highly regarded in the United
States, was relatively unknown in Germany. Its name,
though, which had a definite American sound, turned
out to be a real drawback as the German consumers
disliked the American association.[3] Similarly, in the
early 1960s General Mills spent over $1.4 million ad-
vertising its Betty Crocker cake mixes in an effort to
gain entry into the British market. The costly promotion, though, did not achieve the expected positive
results either. Although research revealed that the
product itself was quite acceptable, the British just
could not identify with the exotic names given to the
cake mixes.[4]

Name adaptations sometimes prove to be winners;
other times they do not. The Johnson Wax Company
successfully introduced its product "Pledge" in Germany under the name of "Pronto," but problems
arose when the product entered the market in the
Netherlands as "Pliz." In Dutch, the pronunciation of
"Pliz" sounds like "Piss." Understandably, it was
rather difficult for the customer of the conventional
Dutch grocery store to ask for the product.

Sometimes the required change in the product
name is a rather simple one. Wrigley, for example,
merely altered the spelling of its "Spearmint" chew-
ing gum to "Speermint" to aid in the German pronunciation of the flavor. "Maxwell House" proved
slightly more difficult. The name was changed to
"Maxwell Kaffee" in Germany, "Legal" in France,
and "Monky" in Spain.

As evidenced, firms have blundered by changing
product names and by failing to alter names. This is

not to say, however, that one is "damned if you do and damned if you don't." Adequate name assessments prior to market introduction can reduce potential name blunders.

More obscene meanings

Inappropriate product names sometimes prove to be quite humorous, but in a number of cases, the names have actually borne fairly obscene implications and connotations. A few illustrations of this type of blunder are cited below.

Bird's Eye considered itself quite fortunate when it discovered that a proposed name for one of its fish-food products was inappropriate. Wisely, the company decided against the name when it uncovered that the name translated to "genitals." Not all firms have been so lucky. A well-known oil company was caught in an embarrassing situation when it learned of the "indecent" name it had chosen for its products. The company established operations in Indonesia and manufactured machinery displaying the name "Nonox." One can imagine the firm's discomfort when it was informed that "Nonox" sounded similar to the Javanese slang word *Nonok* which is comparable to the American idiom for female "private parts."

Obviously the employees who proposed the name "Joni" for a new facial cream which was to be marketed in India had never read the erotic Indian classic *Kama Sutra.* If they had, they would surely have known that the Hindu word *joni* represents the most intimate areas of the female body.

The example of a vitamin product introduced in South America serves as a final illustration of how

product names can unintentionally become obsceni-
ties. In this case, a company introduced its vitamins
as "Fundavit" and boasted that they satisfied the fun-
damental vitamin requirements. The name had to be
modified when the firm learned that "fundola" in
Spanish stands for the rear end of an attractive young
female.

Other offensive names

As illustrated, certain product name choices can
create embarrassing situations for companies when
the names are interpreted as indecencies. On occasion, a company chooses a name which, although not
obscene, turns out to be in poor taste and offensive
to certain groups of people. One example is the name
"Black Nikka" chosen for a brand of Japanese whis-
key sold in the United States and found to be de-
meaning by some black Americans. Also consider the
bold experiment in international marketing that
brought together the state-controlled tobacco monop-
olies of five countries (France, Italy, Portugal, Austria, and Japan) to launch a major promotion of a
new brand of cigarettes, "Champagne." This venture
proved to be an embarrassment to the French government, and the case wound up in the international law
courts with the French champagne producers in a
fury. These producers claimed that the use of "Champagne" as a brand name "is deplorable, and the connection with health hazards may permanently damage
our image."[5]

Yves St. Laurent drew some unwanted criticism
when it named a new fragrance "Opium." Even
though the advertising campaign was voted the best
for 1978 by the Fragrance Foundation, it created a
storm of protest. In general, it was simply viewed as

poor judgment to name a fragrance after an illegal drug. The original French slogan "Pour celles qui s'adonnet á Yves St. Laurent" ("For those who are addicted to Yves St. Laurent") only tended to reinforce the resented "connections" and connotations. The Chinese also considered the use of the name "Opium" to be a racial slur. Public pressure eventually forced the company to discontinue the sales promotion in some places.[6] Therefore, it can not be stressed too strongly: Names must be chosen carefully.

COMPANY NAMES

Product names are not the only ones which can generate company blunders. If a firm name is misinterpreted or incorrectly translated, it too can cause the same types of humorous, obscene, offensive, or unexpected situations. A number of examples are described in the following paragraphs.

A private Egyptian airline, Misair, proved to be rather unpopular with the French nationals. Could the fact that the name, when pronounced, meant "misery" in French have contributed to the airline's plight? Another airline trying to gain acceptance in Australia only complicated matters when it chose the firm name "EMU." The emu is an Australian bird which is incapable of flying. But EMU was not the only company to run into snags while conducting business in Australia. The AMF Corporation was forced to change its name. Why? Because AMF is the official designation for the Australian military forces. Similarly, Sears was forbidden to use its unchanged name in Spain. The company commanded respect and had developed a good reputation there, but since the

Castillian Spanish pronunciation of Sears sounded much like "Seat" (the name of Spain's largest car manufacturer), Seat forced Sears to incorporate the name "Roebuck" on all of its products.

When Esso realized that its name phonetically meant "stalled car," it understood why it had had difficulties in the Japanese market. And was it any wonder that Ford ran into unexpected low sales levels in Spain? Apparently its cars were not popular with certain groups; some of the locals were interpreting the name "Ford" to mean "*F*abrica *O*rdinaria *R*eparaciones *D*iaviamente" (translation: "ordinarily, make repairs daily"). The Vicks Company, however, was more fortunate. It discovered that in German "Vicks" sounds like the most crude slang equivalent of intercourse and was able to change its name to an acceptable "Wicks."

As a final illustration, consider the trade magazine which promoted giftware and launched a worldwide circulation effort. The magazine used the word *gift* in its title and as part of its name. When it was later revealed that *gift* is the German word for *poison,* a redfaced publishing executive supposedly retorted that the Germans should simply find a new word for poison!

Of course not all companies have been forced to change names. In fact, some of them have traveled quite well. Kodak may be the most famous example. A research team deliberately "developed" this name after carefully searching for a word which was pronounceable everywhere but had no specific meaning anywhere. Exxon is another such name which was reportedly accepted only after a lengthy and expensive computer-assisted search.

SUMMARY

Multinational corporations have experienced many unexpected troubles concerning company or product names, and even attempts to alter names have led to blunders. It should be evident that careful planning and study of the potential market are necessary as name adaptation can be every bit as important as product or package modification.

4 PROMOTION

In the field of marketing, product promotion has caused the most corporate headaches. The old adage, "if something can go wrong, it will," seems especially true for promoters. At some point in time, someone has undoubtedly blundered every single promotional task imaginable.

Timing is one of the most critical elements in the launching of a new product. Most firms understand this and also recognize that various peoples hold different conceptions of time. Since some nationalities are more conscious of time factors than others, extra time must often be allocated to assure that everything is completed as scheduled. One firm aware of these constraints properly timed everything, or so it thought. Various types of promotional activities were arranged, but one thing was overlooked—the product. Because someone forgot to assure its availability, all of the expensive, well-planned promotions became meaningless.

In another case, a company formed a joint venture with an Asian firm. Both companies believed everything to be in order. Their plan included a large production run and a simultaneous, large promotional effort. Production went well, but the expected promotional efforts never materialized. Each company had assumed that the other would coordinate and pay for all promotional efforts. In fact, each firm simply assumed the customs of its own country's business practices and was not prepared to accept the other country's norm. Neither company would have agreed to the venture had it thought that it would be responsible for promotion costs. The promotion was never undertaken, and the joint venture eventually broke up.[1]

One American corporation believed it had developed a good promotional plan when it decided to distribute simulated old coins displaying the company logo. To make the coins appear a bit more realistic, the company placed a monetary value on them and, to avoid any chance of claims of counterfeiting, it used the obviously phony value of $1 billion. The coins were passed out at a trade show in West Germany but, to the company's surprise, the coins seemed to anger the locals. Apparently the Germans felt that the company was trying to show off American wealth, and they resented this impression. The coins would have been much more effective if they had displayed some denomination of the German mark.

As the women's movement continues to gain momentum, more and more firms are realizing they must scrutinize all promotional efforts carefully to make sure that their advertisements are not offensive to women. Failure to recognize potential problems can cause later difficulties (such as product boycotts). Quebec, for example, now has a review board which monitors possibly offensive advertisements. In 1981, it presented its first "awards" for sexism. One "award" was conferred for a Sony and La Place stereo shop ad. The ad portrayed a big-busted woman with her nipples showing through her T-shirt as she roller skated holding her Sony tape deck. The review jury found that since there was no connection between the woman and the product being advertised, such a picture was offensive. Another "award" went to Procter & Gamble for its 30-second Mr. Clean television commercial. In this ad, a little girl is shown cleaning up her brother's mess as he watches without making an effort to help. The jury felt the company was reinforcing the old role stereotypes that housecleaning is women's work and that women should serve men.[2]

Promotional efforts often misfire; some downfalls, though, are more predictable than others. In Japan, a cosmetics firm attempted to sell its lipstick through a television ad which depicted Nero coming to life just as a pretty woman wearing the lipstick strolled by. This hard sell was resented by the Japanese women who had no real idea of who Nero was.[3] If a firm decides to use historical figures in promotional campaigns, it is well advised to first consider using locally known historical figures.

In Chapter 2, the problem of using inappropriate product and package colors was discussed. Colors, however, create promotional difficulties as well. The Singer Company, for example, had to halt an elaborate outdoor ad campaign, when, just prior to its introduction, the company discovered that the background color, blue, was the local color representing death. Things could have turned out worse for Singer, of course, if the error hadn't been detected when it was. Because Singer had hired local people to implement its promotional plan, the potential blunder was averted.

The McDonnell Douglas Corporation experienced unexpected difficulties with a brochure to be distributed to potential aircraft customers in India. The promotional material depicted turbaned men, but the photos were not well received. The company had used old *National Geographic* pictures and had overlooked the fact that the turbans were being worn by Pakistani men—not Indians!

If a theme works exceedingly well in one country, then naturally it becomes very tempting for a firm to want to use it elsewhere. The risks involved in doing this are high, however, because good themes many times are culturally oriented. Consider the very popular and successful Marlboro advertisements. The Marlboro man projects a strong masculine image in America and in Europe, but not everywhere. Attempts to use it were unsuccessful in Hong Kong, where the totally urban people did not identify at all with horseback riding in the countryside. So Philip Morris quickly changed its ad to reflect a Hong Kong-style Marlboro man. He is still a virile cowboy, but he is younger, better dressed, and owns a truck and the land he's on.

Local weather conditions can also foul up a multinational corporation's promotional campaign. One firm, for example, tried to use a typical U.S.-type radio advertisement to promote its swim suits in Latin America. The ad boasted that one could wear the swim suit all day in the sun and it would not fade. The local Latins, however, were unable to understand this point because the weather is always too hot to stay in the sun for very long.

Conducting business with a Communist country is especially tricky. A slip of the tongue or pen can be fatal. Even the name of the country can cause troubles since the names given to Eastern countries by the West are usually different than those used by the Eastern countries themselves. The failure to use the proper country name is often considered an insensitive or offensive act. For instance, the English-language catalog of a Swedish firm had to be changed because the catalog cited "North Korea" instead of the "People's Republic of Korea." Similarly, another catalog used in China had to be altered when it listed "North Vietnam." One company's promotional brochure stated that it had representatives in 100 countries and then proceeded to list Hong Kong as one of them. The snag here was that the People's Republic of China insists that Hong Kong is a colony rather than a country.

Several firms have tried to use old, reliable promotional methods in countries where they simply do not work. Billboard advertisements are perfectly legal in most parts of the Middle East, for example, but this does not mean one should use them. Many companies have tried to use billboards, but instead of advertising their product, they have merely exposed their lack of awareness of local weather conditions. In the Middle East environment, billboards often last less than two weeks.

Companies have even been known to promote their products in the wrong language. In Dubai, for example, only 10 percent of the population speaks Arabic. The remaining 90 percent originate from Pakistan, India, Iran, or elsewhere. Several European and American firms, however, have assumed that all Middle Eastern countries are primarily populated with Arabic-speaking people and so have only promoted their products in Arabic.

MISUNDERSTANDINGS

In many cases, the language of the promotional effort is correct, but it is simply not effective. It is one thing to use the right language, but it is quite another to use it so that the intended message is properly communicated. As a classic illustration, consider the company that rented space on a wall beside the main road leading from the airport into Buenos Aires. The following message was placed on the wall, "Par (brand name) vous y seriez deja" which means "with (brand name) you'd be there already." Just one slight problem existed: The message was misunderstood because it was written on a cemetery wall![4]

It may be easy to place a message in the wrong location, but Amalie Refining was off by quite a few miles. One of its Spanish-language billboards somehow landed along the roadside in Knoxville, Tennessee, years before the 1982 World's Fair!

A different type of locational error was committed by a firm at an international trade fair. In order to keep people out of a certain area of its booth, the company displayed a sign depicting an open, flat hand with all fingers pointing up on the swinging door which led to the restricted area. To the company's surprise, its idea backfired. The local people interpreted the symbol to mean they should place their hands there and push open the door.

Symbols or logos have caused troubles for other companies as well. A U.S. firm marketing in Brazil found itself a bit embarrassed when it used a large deer as a sign for masculinity. The word *deer* is a Brazilian street name for a homosexual. Another company blundered in India when it used an owl in its promotional efforts. To an Indian, the owl is a symbol for bad luck, and indeed it proved to be just that for the firm.

A Japanese steel firm, Sumitomo, recently introduced its specialty steel pipe into the U.S. market. Sumitomo used a Tokyo-based, Japanese agency to help develop its advertisements. The steel was named "*S*umitomo *H*igh *T*oughness," and the name was promoted by the acronym SHT in bold letters. So bold, in fact, that the full-page ads run in trade journals were three fourths filled with SHT. Located at the bottom of the page was a short message which ended with the claim that the product "was made to match its name." It simply cannot be overemphasized that local input is vital.

One laundry detergent company certainly wishes now that it had contacted a few locals before it initiated its promotional campaign in the Middle East. All of the company's advertisements pictured soiled clothes on the left, its box of soap in the middle, and clean clothes on the right. But, because in that area of the world people tend to read from the right to the left, many potential customers interpreted the message to indicate the soap actually soiled the clothes.

Even if the proper words are used and spaced appropriately, problems can crop up due to incorrect intonation. Missionaries in Africa discovered this when someone finally informed them that their songs were being misunderstood. The words were correctly translated, but the tones and pitches had been sung erroneously for years. For example, the Igbo people of Nigeria had learned to sing the second verse of "Oh, Come All Ye Faithful." They were thought to be singing "Very God, begotten not created," but the actual meaning was "God's pig, which is never shared." Another hymn with words of "There is no sorrow in heaven," came out "There is no egg on the bicycle."

Care must be taken even when the consumers of the foreign market speak the same language. A British and U.S. joint venture proposal ran into serious difficulties, for example, when the U.S. firm requested that certain key points be "tabled." The British firm agreed and both parties prepared for the negotiations. When the British team brought up for discussion those topics which had been "tabled," both parties became highly irritated. It seems that in the United States "to table a motion" means to avoid discussion of it, but in England, the same phrase often means to bring the topic to the table for discussion. The Americans had requested the exact opposite of what they had really wanted.

Similar problems were encountered by another U.S. company attempting to conduct business in Britain. The firm had effectively used the phrase "You can use no finer napkin at your dinner table" in the United States and, due to economies of scale, etc., decided to use the same commercials in England. After all, Britons do speak English. To a Briton, however, an American does not speak English, but speaks "American" and uses different phrases and word meanings. Since the British word *napkin* or *nappy* actually means *diaper*, the American firm was unknowingly advertising that "You could use no finer diaper at your dinner table." The ad was entertaining, but could hardly be expected to boost sales greatly.

American troubles with the English language are not limited to England, of course. One U.S. banker in Australia discovered this when he attended an important dinner given in his honor. He was invited to speak after the meal, but he certainly began on the wrong foot when he indicated that he was "full." The subsequent nervous laughter of the other diners suggested something was wrong, so he tried to clarify the situation by saying that he was "stuffed." One can imagine his astonishment when he was informed that "full" implied being drunk and that "stuffed" indicated being involved in sexual intercourse.

POOR PERSONNEL CHOICES

Just as in any domestic employment position, if a firm places an inappropriate person in an international job, the results can prove disastrous. Several companies have blundered by their placement of culturally insensitive individuals in sensitive management and sales positions overseas. In one case, a firm introduced a technical product into a market relatively free of competition. Believing that market entry would pose no problem, the company did not pay enough attention to the personal characteristics of the man it chose as its European sales manager. This was unfortunate. The individual chosen disliked Frenchmen and made no effort to ingratiate himself or learn their culture or language. His dislike even spilled over to his abrupt treatment of the sales force. A competitor soon came along and was able to take over much of the market and most of the man's original sales force. This illustration points out that personalities definitely play a role in the securing of both brand-name and personnel loyalty.

In the past, U.S. firms have occasionally hired managers for European or Asian posts who have behaved arrogantly and treated others as inferiors. These individuals, displaying indifference to the local norms, have helped build the image of the "Ugly American."

An employee's attitude, however, is not the only variable of importance. A person may have very good intentions but simply not be qualified for the job. Several cases can be cited. A major U.S. appliance manufacturer, for instance, experiencing difficulties in Spain, sent three troubleshooters there to help. The company overlooked one important fact: The individuals could not speak Spanish. After repeated efforts to communicate failed, the Spaniards eventually lost respect for the three specialists. The problems worsened until a Spanish-speaking manager was sent to help. A similar situation occurred in Germany. An American manager who understood little German was sent to West Germany to discuss marketing plans with the local German subsidiary managers. The local managers, however, spoke little English. Both sides tried to understand each other, but neither nationality did very well. Eventually they parted, thinking that all were in agreement. It was later discovered that during the meeting many important points were overlooked, and the company subsequently lost numerous sales opportunities.

Even though a manager maintains the right attitudes and speaks the language, a successful performance is not assured. Raytheon hired Italian-Americans to manage operations in Sicily but found that the strategy was not as effective as hoped. In this case the trouble lay in the origins of the managers. Because their family ties were with the mainland and not Sicilian, they were not trusted or accepted.

An effective expatriate manager must possess special abilities and traits if he or she is to avoid blundering. Among the most important characteristics are:

1. An ability to get along well with people.
2. An awareness of cultural differences.
3. Open-mindedness.
4. Tolerance of foreign cultures.
5. Adaptability to new cultures, ideas, and challenges.
6. An ability to adjust quickly to new conditions.
7. An interest in facts, not blind assumptions.
8. Previous business experience.
9. Previous experience with foreign cultures.
10. An ability to learn foreign languages.

This list is by no means complete. In fact, Business International identifies 60 attributes which a good international executive should possess.[5] With so many necessary characteristics, it is no wonder that business people sometimes make mistakes.

INCORRECT PROMOTIONAL STRATEGY

Often it is the promotional strategy that runs amuck and creates the promotional blunders. Whereas some corporations have appeared culturally insensitive, others have blundered by going to the opposite extreme. They have tried to fake being local or have tried to play up to local nationalistic preferences. In 1963, for instance, Dow Breweries introduced a new beer in Quebec, Canada, called "Kebec." The promotion incorporated the Canadian flag and attempted to evoke nationalistic pride. Dow's strategy backfired, however, when major local groups protested the "profane" use of "sacred" symbols. The campaign was halted within 15 days.

A French beer company experienced difficulty trying to enter the U.S. market when it projected itself as American. Its decision to portray its imported beer as locally brewed was not a wise one because the American market was already flooded with plenty of local beers. The company, realizing its error, now does well promoting its beer as an import.

The perception of the product's characteristics plays an important role in marketing strategy. One must note that the importance of certain product traits varies from country to country. Multinational corporations, therefore, must consider varying promotional tactics. Volvo has applied this concept quite successfully. The company has emphasized economy, durability, and safety in America; status and leisure in France; performance in Germany; and safety in Switzerland. Price is considered to be a critical variable to Mexican consumers, but quality is of more importance to Venezuelans.

Test markets can be used to evaluate promotional campaigns, but results are not necessarily fail-safe. Puerto Rico is often used as a typical Latin American test market by U.S. companies. Although Puerto Rico is a convenient, almost barrier-free, Spanish-speaking market and thus an appealing test market, the natives of each Latin American country have their own unique tastes and preferences. Therefore, firms must realize that the success of a promotional strategy in Puerto Rico does not necessarily assure success in all Latin American countries. All that should be gleaned with confidence from a positive result in Puerto Rico is that the strategy is worth testing in the country under consideration. Major blunders have occurred when this second testing procedure was skipped. The managers of one company, for example, were so excited by the impressive results experienced in Puerto Rico that they shipped large quantities of their product, a hair fixer, to Argentina. Sales were practically nonexistent even though the commercials so successful in Puerto Rico were used. Sales improved only after the local sales manager convinced the company to alter the ads and direct them towards a more European-type customer.

Unilever experienced a somewhat unique type of promotional problem. The company marketed a popular detergent, "Radion," in Germany. It also sold the same basic product in Austria but marketed it under a different brand name. Because Germans and Austrians both speak German and are often exposed to each other's media, consumers in each country were being introduced to what they thought were competitive products. Since the promotional campaigns developed for one country easily reached the consumers in the other country, a more efficient and effective marketing strategy would have been to use the same brand name in both countries. Had this occurred, the promotional overlap would have reinforced efforts and helped sales.

Two well-known authorities of multinational marketing report that five steps are involved in the development of a good promotional strategy:

1. Determine the blend of advertising, personal selling, and sales promotion for each country.
2. Determine the amount of worldwide standardization.

3. Develop the messages.

4. Select the media.

5. Establish the necessary controls.[6]

As might be expected, steps 3 and 5 have caused more blunders 'than any of the others, but mistakes have been made during the establishment of each step. Those mistakes least understandable but most avoidable have involved the first two steps.

One fairly common American practice is that of utilizing the same promotional strategy for all domestic subsidiaries. Promotional budgets many times are based on a fixed-percentage-of-sales basis. This strategy often works well with domestic ventures but usually proves foolish when it is attempted for overseas subsidiaries as well. U.S. companies which try to force such standardization are often asking their foreign managers to do the impossible. For one thing, some types of media are not legally available. In many countries, no television advertisements are permitted. This, alone, makes a U.S.-style promotional budget infeasible. A second problem is one of scale. The use of a standard percentage of sales may be appropriate for large, domestic subsidiaries, but for small foreign subsidiaries, 10 percent may not support a single promotional campaign. Several companies have attempted standardized promotional budgets, but most have now realized that each market provides different opportunities and challenges at different cost structures. A better strategy is to standardize the methods used to analyze opportunities and the methods used to develop local promotional budgets. Subsidiaries can then be urged to follow the established methods during the development of their own promotional budgets.[7]

CULTURAL DIFFERENCES

Dozens of blunders have been made by firms that failed to study local customs carefully. As one example, consider the public display of physical contact between members of opposite sexes. In many countries, this is totally unacceptable and offensive. Thailand is one of these countries. A firm trying to introduce its mouthwash there, however, was not aware of this norm and promoted its product through an ad that displayed a young couple holding hands. By changing the advertisement to feature two women, the commercials were deemed acceptable and no longer offensive to the Thais.

The Asian Indians found a BiNoca Talc ad disturbing even though the woman in the advertisement was wearing a body stocking. The promotion, appearing in many of the major local newspapers, featured an attractive but apparently nude young woman lavishly splashing herself with BiNoca's talcum powder. Strategic portions of her body were carefully covered with the slogan "Don't go wild—just enough is all you need of BiNoca talc." The public, however, was not prepared for the ad's use of the female form and found the ads extremely indecent.

In other countries, such exposure is not deemed as offensive. In fact, the French, more than many nationalities, accept commercials that feature a great deal of the female body. But there are norms for each country, and sometimes they are very strict.

To some groups, the display of certain parts of the body generally believed harmless proves to be offensive. One American shoe manufacturer promoted its product through photos of bare feet. Although considered a harmless ad by many, the photos were shown in Southeast Asia where exposure of the foot is considered an insult.

Mountain Bell experienced a similar problem when one of its promotional photos depicted an executive talking on the telephone with his feet propped up on his desk. The photos, seen by Middle and Far Easterners, were considered to be in poor taste. To them, the display of the sole of the foot or shoe is one of the worst possible insults.

Since social norms vary so greatly from country to country, it is extremely difficult for any outsider to be knowledgeable of them all. As pointed out previously, local input can be vital in avoiding blunders. Many promotional errors could have been averted had this warning been heeded.

One of the best-known promotional blunders occurred in Quebec. In this instance, a manufacturer of canned fish ran advertisements in the local newspapers which depicted a woman in shorts playing golf with a man. The caption explained that a woman could go golfing with her husband in the afternoon and still get home in time to serve a great dinner of canned fish that same evening. The entire promotional effort was off target. Women did not wear shorts on local golf courses and were not usually permitted to golf with men. Furthermore, regardless of how much time for preparation was available, women would not have considered serving canned fish for dinner, especially as the main course. The company seems to have completely neglected to consider local customs, and obviously the product failed.[8]

Pepsodent reportedly tried to sell its toothpaste in regions of Southeast Asia through a promotion which stressed that the toothpaste helped enhance white teeth. In this area, where some local people deliberately chewed betel nut in order to achieve the social prestige of darkly stained teeth, such an ad was understandably less than effective. The slogan "wonder where the yellow went" was also viewed by many as a racial slur.

Drawing by Stephen Foster

The above cartoon was used to illustrate the "Pepsodent" problem when the author was on the "Today Show" to talk about international business blunders.

A marketer of eyeglasses promoted his spectacles in Thailand with commercials featuring animals wearing glasses. It was an unfortunate decision, however. Animals there are considered a low life form, and it is beneath humans to wear anything worn by an animal.

The failure to consider specialized aspects of local religions has created a number of difficulties for firms. Companies have encountered problems in Asia when they incorporated a picture of a Buddha in their promotions. Religious ties are strong in this area, and the use of local religious symbols in advertising is strongly resented—especially when words are deliberately or even accidentally printed across the picture of a Buddha. One company was nearly burned to the ground when it ignorantly tried such a strategy. The seemingly minor incident led to a major international political conflict remembered for years.

Another religious-type blunder occurred when a refrigerator manufacturer used a picture of a refrigerator containing a centrally placed chunk of ham. The typical refrigerator advertisement often features a refrigerator full of delicious food, and because these photos are difficult to take, the photos are generally used in as many places as possible. This company used its stock photo one place too many, though, when it was used in the Middle East where Moslems do not eat ham. Locals considered the ad to be insensitive and unappealing.

An entertainment promoter also encountered difficulties when he failed to recognize one of the Moslem mores. He had booked Anita Sarawak in Singapore, and during her performance, encouraged her to hold her pet dog while singing "Me and You and a Dog Named Boo." This gimmick had worked well in other countries but caused a major commotion in Singapore. Plans for subsequent taped broadcasts of the show were cancelled, all because of the dog. According to Islamic beliefs, dogs are dirty and should not be shown or kept as pets.

Saudi Arabia nearly restricted an airline from initiating flights when the company authorized "normal" newspaper advertisements. The ads featured attractive hostesses serving champagne to the happy airline passengers. Because in Saudi Arabia alcohol is illegal and unveiled women are not permitted to mix with men, the photo was viewed as an attempt to alter religious customs.

As stated earlier, successful advertisements usually involve cultural assumptions, so using the same commercial in more than one country can be dangerous. Cosmetics firms in the United States, for example, often pitch their messages to flatter the American woman's ego by telling her how attractive she is or will be if she uses their products. Similar commercials have been introduced in France and have failed. French women do not identify themselves as being ultra glamorous nor do they believe that they can be. Often they do not even realize that the commercial is aimed at them, and so they simply assume that the message must be intended for a rare few.

A major cereal company reportedly experienced problems with its breakfast food commercials when it implemented a promotional strategy in Britain similar to the one used in America. The American ads often featured children and aimed the messages at them. Even the packages pictured the typical freckled, red-haired American kid. The British, however, resented both the use of the children in the promotion and the company's attempt to influence children. They considered it improper to aim a sales pitch at a child and forced the firm to create totally new commercials directed toward adults. Although the company originally named in the report now denies that it was involved, the conclusion remains the same: Awareness of local cultural norms is critical.

Cultural norms include the accepted methods of presenting information. In the Orient, for example, a person should not try to make the other "lose face." But to be taken seriously in Italy, a person must try to win the argument. A person speaking precisely will be taken literally in Switzerland. The British prefer a much "softer sell" than the Germans.[9]

As mentioned previously, the choosing of a color is another important task. At least two different firms encountered problems in their Hong Kong marketing efforts when they decided to use green hats in commercials. One company attempted to sell its beer using the message that the beer was so good that even the Irish like it. The Irishman, of course, wore a green hat while drinking his beer. The other firm marketed cleaning agents and in its commercial featured individuals tossing hats at a male model. A green hat eventually landed on the man. In both cases, the color chosen was not appropriate; the green hat is a Chinese symbol used to identify a man as a cuckold. Understandably, both products were avoided.

As Guiness Stout can attest, Hong Kong has been the site of more than one unexpected turn of events. This firm's thick brew, considered especially well suited for the virile men of the British empire, had somehow achieved a reputation in Hong Kong as being an excellent drink for women during pregnancy or menstrual periods. Consequently, when the drink was promoted in Hong Kong as one for men, it elicited much laughter. Any man ordering it was likely to be asked if it was his "time of the month!"

Another unusual problem occurred in Peru when a laundry detergent containing stain-removing enzymes was introduced through a cartoon depicting large-mouthed enzymes eating the dirt off of clothes. Although sales levels were initially good, they quickly dropped off. A local Peruvian custom was at the base of the company's problem. Peruvian women believed that they must boil their clothes to kill the germs, and the voracious cartoon creatures in the ad reinforced this belief. However, because the boiling destroyed the enzymes, the detergent was boiled to a useless state and did not perform as advertised. As a result, since the product was not as effective as expected, the women only tried it once.

Not all companies find their products are being used correctly, but sometimes unusual uses do not hurt sales. Gervais Danone, for example, was able to turn the tables on a potential problem. The company, finding that the Mexicans had little interest in its products, decided to alter its promotional strategy. It found that it was eventually able to interest the adults in using its cheeses for butter and its Petite Swisse, a creamy whipped cheese, as a good snack for the children.

The Latin market in the United States

Not all cultural problems occur outside the multinational corporation's home country. For example, a significant Latin market exists in the United States, and it is becoming increasingly obvious that companies need to be aware of Latin culture. Sometimes it is even worthwhile to develop separate and special promotional campaigns aimed at this market. Colgate Palmolive, for example, has been able to promote its toothpaste effectively within the Hispanic community through ads which place less emphasis on health and more emphasis on appearance. Not all companies are so successful, however. Several examples of misses or near misses in promotional efforts are cited in the following paragraphs.

A telephone company tried to incorporate a Latin flavor in its commercial by employing Puerto Rican actors. In the ad, the wife said to her husband, "Run downstairs and phone Mary. Tell her we'll be a little late." This commercial contained two major cultural errors: Latin wives seldom dare order their husbands around, and almost no Latin would feel it necessary to phone to warn of tardiness since it is expected.

Coors commercials promoting the slogan "Taste the high country" featured people enjoying Coors beer and life in the Rocky Mountains. This approach, very effective with Anglo-Americans, did not appeal to Mexican-Americans who could not identify with mountain life. Therefore, the Spanish language ads were modified. The mountains were identified as a good source of beer, but one did not necessarily need to live in the mountains to enjoy the beer or to be happy. The new slogan, in its English version, became "Take the beer from the high country and bring it to your high country—wherever it may be."

Johnson and Johnson discovered a potential cultural blunder in time. The firm was set to promote its disposable diapers through advertisements containing references to a mother's wet lap and a father's being dry when it was uncovered that such phrases bore indelicate sexual references in the Hispanic market. This discovery was fortunate for the company since such an ad would have created a great deal of embarrassment and would have drawn unwanted attention.

Pedro Domeca wines also averted a mishap. It was about to use the slogan "the art of simpatico drinking" to promote Spanish wines. A U.S. advertising agency had created the slogan which was intended to tie together the Spanish wine and the favorable U.S. translation and use of the word "simpatico." However, the Spanish do not use the word with the same connotation. The correct Spanish usage is "El es muy simpatico" (He is very likable, agreeable, genial). Since, in Spanish, "simpatico" always refers to a person and never to drinking, the promotional campaign would have seemed foolish to the Spanish-speaking community. Fortunately, some Spanish-speaking managers from Pedro Domeca revealed this error in time.[10]

LEGAL

Most countries have now established regulations dealing with advertising. As many companies can avow, the failure to follow these guidelines almost always results in a legal dispute.

Singapore's airline is one company that can attest to this. It placed advertisements in local Norwegian magazines featuring a photo of a girl's face on a pillow. The message essentially said "Bring me a pillow and brandy for a tired father." The Norwegians were upset with the ad, and the promotion was ruled misleading and sexually discriminating.

To promote its "3T" tire in a number of countries,

Goodyear used its U.S. advertising copy. The ad demonstrated the strength of the "3T" by featuring the tire breaking a chain. In several of the countries, including the United States, the campaign was effective. The firm encountered legal problems in West Germany, however, because German law dictates that superlatives are not permitted. One product can not be called better (or stronger) than another. At last word, the company was still appealing the ruling.

The use of a commercial featuring a bikini-clad woman also created difficulties for Goodyear. In several of the countries where the commercial was shown, such attire was not locally permitted. The company was forced to alter the scene and replace the young beauty with fully dressed people having fun. The message, "Get where the fun is," remained unchanged, but it was much more acceptable and effective.

Claridge cigarettes advertised its product in Australia with a campaign that featured Robin Hood and Friar Tuck. Australians, believing that their children might find the ad appealing, felt that this was an inappropriate orientation and forced Claridge to alter its advertisement.

Ford experienced a similar problem with one of its ads shown in Norway. The promotion featured children talking to a car salesman with a caption which read, "Is it true that there is a waiting period for Fords?" Local groups complained it was improper to use children when they presented no direct connection to the product. While such usage as this could easily be considered harmless and enjoyable by many, a firm must consider potential legal expenses should it find itself defending its ads.

A novel twist occurred in France where Philip Morris, Inc. and the R. J. Reynolds Tobacco Co. were enjoying much financial success. The companies, in fact, were so successful that a local company, SEITA, tried to sell its cigarettes as if they, too, were foreign imports. Their packages bore the name "News" and were printed totally in English. Not even the well-known French name of the parent company was listed. This, however, was against French law, and so, in at least this one case, it was the local company that experienced the legal difficulties in its effort to thwart foreign competition.[11]

SUMMARY

This chapter has introduced a number of problems encountered when companies attempted to promote products in international markets. Blunders have been made in all types of media and for a wide variety of reasons. Both simple and complex misunderstandings have led to difficulties. Sometimes mistakes arose from human error or the use of culturally insensitive persons. On occasion, an entire promotional strategy has proved foolish. In many cases, the blunders were simply the result of the company's failure to understand cultural differences, some basic but some more subtle. A few problems encountered were based upon differences in regulations. With so many different kinds of potential blunders, it is easy to believe that every promotional task imaginable has been bungled at one time or another by someone, someplace.

5 TRANSLATION

Translation errors are the cause of a great number and variety of international business blunders. In fact, the largest subset of promotional blunders is the category of mistakes that have arisen through faulty translations. There are three basic categories of translation errors: simple carelessness, multiple-meaning words, and idioms. All three types are described and discussed in this chapter as well as details about the various ways in which the likelihood of translation blunders can be lessened.

CARELESSNESS

The careless rendition of advertising or promotional messages into other languages has been found to be the most prevalent type of translation blunder. Obviously, these mistakes can often result in an embarrassing or damaging situation. The first two examples reported below illustrate how errors made in product promotion can directly injure overseas sales.

An automobile manufacturer had promoted its product in an English-speaking market by declaring that its product "topped them all." This may have been so, but the French Canadians would not have known. When the product was introduced, the phrase was mistranslated in French. The result: the company actually boasted that its cars were "topped by them all." Another American manufacturer in the auto industry advertised its auto battery as "highly rated." Unfortunately, when the company introduced its product in Venezuela, the battery was described as "highly overrated." Here again the company had used a thoughtless translation of a key promotional phrase. Needless to say, sales did not boom in either case./

Careless translations can prove to be humorous to the consumer and/or embarrassing to the firm. Consider, for example, the experience of the Otis Engineering Corporation when it participated in an exhibition held in Moscow. Initially, the company's representatives could not discern why its display won Soviet snickers as well as praise. Much to their disappointment and embarrassment, it was discovered that a careless translator had rendered a sign which identified "completion equipment" as "equipment for orgasms."

On the opposite side of the globe, another firm was experiencing the headaches caused by a poor translator. In this case, a Mexican-magazine promotion for an American-brand shirt carried a message stating the exact opposite of what had originally been intended. The advertisement, instead of declaring "when I used this shirt, I felt good," read "until I used this shirt, I felt good."

Many a small business has thwarted its own efforts through the use of poor translation. For example, one business person, trying to save a bit of money, hired an Indonesian exchange student to translate the instruction book of a computer destined for Jakarta. Not surprisingly, the student did not understand computer terminology, so the computer "software" was translated as "underwear." The manual must have provided interesting reading!

In efforts to attract tourists and foreign business people, other small businesses have created some rather funny situations. For instance, a department store in Thailand posted a sign which read "Visit our bargain basement one flight up." Another misguided individual in Thailand tried to attract business with a sign asking "Would you like to ride on your ass?" And in Japan, an interesting but misleading translation showed up on a sign in a Japanese garden. The posted sign read, "Japanese garden is the mental home of the Japanese."

A firm in the Middle East was able to attract attention, but not exactly the kind it had hoped for. It seems that a Saudi Arabian laundry had posted, in English, a list of its cleaning prices. It was not its prices, though, that were attracting people. The company had used a poor translator, and among the many spelling errors on the poster was the omission of the letter *r* in "lady's shirt." One can imagine the customers' reactions! Another laundry, this time a hotel laundry in Tokyo, also experienced an embarrassing situation. The hotel's instructions, translated into English, stated, "The flattening of underwear with pressure is the job of the chambermaid. To get it done, turn her on." One suspects that the message was literally translated, but obviously it is not to be taken this way. It is easy to understand the importance of an accurate translation and the negative results possible if this work is not done carefully.

One of the more unusual errors made by a small business occurred in Kowloon. A sign in the hotel read, "It is forbidden to steal hotel towels, please if you are not person to do such is please not to read notice." What one can assume from this is that someone tried to communicate in another language, but with a bit of difficulty. Sometimes it might be best not to try to translate at all. More on this will be discussed later in the chapter.

To conclude this section dealing with careless translation errors, consider only one area of the world— Quebec. Quebec has been the site of a number of corporate blunders, most of them due to simple carelessness. There is no reason, for example, for a firm to have used the words *lavement d'auto* (car enema) instead of the correct *lavage d'auto* (car wash), but one firm did. Another company boasted of "lait frais usage" (used fresh milk) when it meant to brag of "lait frais employe" (fresh milk used). The "terrific" pens of one firm were promoted as "terrifiantes" (terrifying) instead. Indeed, such a poor translation is terrifying! One company, intending to report that its appliance would use any kind of electrical current, actually stated that the appliance wears out any kind of liquid. And imagine how one company felt when its product to reduce heartburn was advertised as one that reduced warmth of heart. Yet another unfortunate firm claimed that its product was a stumbling block to success when it really wanted to claim that its product provided a stepping stone to success.

Obviously, errors are fairly easy to make and perhaps understandable when something as seemingly insignificant as an accent mark can alter a message considerably. One promotion, for example, which was supposed to relay "Don't be half-sure, be PONKO-sure," declared instead "Ne Soyex pas DEMI-SUR, soyez PONKO-SUR." At the root of this translation mishap was the word *sur*. *Sûr* means *sure*, but if the accent mark over the *u* is left off, the word *sur* takes on the meaning *sour*. The company, therefore, was saying "Don't be half-sour, be PONKO sour."

A similar omission of an accent mark created difficulties for yet another company. An American firm hoped to surprise its Mexican-based employees with a New Year's Eve party. Preparations were complete—including balloons with printed slogans (in Spanish) declaring "Happy New Year." However, the accent mark over the "n" in "año" was left off. Without the mark, the word appeared to read "anos" (anus in Spanish). Happy New Anus? Needless to say, the balloons came down before midnight!

All of these blunders point out that even the smallest translation error can greatly affect the intended message and the market's reaction to that message. Occasionally it may only be one seemingly insignificant letter that can change the entire context of the copy. Consider one international corporation that had its annual report translated into Spanish. In the sentence "Our vast enterprise achieved record sales . . . ," the word *vast* was translated into *basto*. The actual Spanish word is *vasto*, but people often become confused because the letters *b* and *v* are pronounced similarly. Due to this error in translation, however, the entire meaning of the sentence was modified to "our crude and uncultured enterprise achieved record sales . . . ."

MULTIPLE MEANINGS

The second category of translation blunders involves translated messages that can convey more than one meaning. The trials and tribulations experienced by the Parker Pen Company can serve as an excellent illustration of how an innocent translation of a multiple-meaning word or phrase can create complex problems. In its advertisements destined for Latin America, Parker had hoped to use the word *bola* to describe its ballpoint pen. However, it was discovered that the word conveys different meanings in different Latin countries. To some, "bola" conveys the intended meaning of "ball," while in another country, the translation means "revolution." "Bola" represents an obscenity in a third country, and in yet another, it means a "lie" or "fabrication." Luckily, the firm was able to uncover this translation problem before it could ever become a blunder.

The company, however, was not so fortunate during its initial product introduction in some parts of Latin America. The Parker Pen Company had developed and promoted in the United States one of the first truly reliable fountain pens. The pen could be carried in a person's shirt without concern regarding the possibility of embarrassing ink stains. The advertisements (and the pens) performed so well that the Parker Pen became quite well known. Eventually, the promotion was shortened to convey that Parker Pens avoid embarrassment. Because this condensed version of the promotional slogan was so successful over time, the older expanded message was taken for granted and basically forgotten. Later, when the firm decided to enter the Latin American market, it merely translated the same condensed promotional slogan then being used in the United States: "Avoid embarrassment—use Parker Pens." The company even posted metal signs featuring this short message on the buildings in which its pens were sold, but the results of the company's promotional efforts were not as anticipated. What had gone wrong? The company had promoted a slogan which contained a multiple-meaning word. The Spanish word for *embarrassment* was also used to indicate pregnancy, so the Parker Pen Company was unknowingly promoting its pens as contraceptives! [1]

An American toothpaste manufacturer also experienced pains with its "pregnancy." The company promised its customers that they would be more "interesting" if they used the firm's toothpaste. What the advertising coordinators did not realize, however, was that in some Latin American countries "interesting" is another euphemism for "pregnant."

Continuing with problems of pregnancy, consider the case of a free-lance Arabic translator who translated an American computer manual into his native language. When confronted with the term *dummy load,* a specialized electronics term, he consulted his dictionary and found the equivalents of "dummy" and "load." When he put these two together, he produced the Arabic term for "false pregnancy."

The Spanish had a good laugh when Chrysler Corporation tried to promote its successful U.S. slogan, "Dart is Power." It seems that the translated version of this message implied that drivers of the car needed sexual vigor. Because of the nearby trees and buildings blocking out the hot sun, a bar in Thailand innocently advertised that it was "the shadiest cocktail bar in Bangkok."

Such double-meaning translation errors can be humorous but are often also embarrassing to the firms involved. One company caught in this situation was granted the dubious distinction of winning *Playboy* magazine's annual "Booby-Boo-Boo Award." Apparently when Hunt-Wesson introduced the Big John family brand in Canada it experienced a bit of difficulty with the French translation. The name, translated as "Gros Jos," also turned out to be a colloquial

French expression which denoted a woman with large breasts. In this case the company was fortunate. Its sales were not badly hurt for a number of men wanted to order the "Gros Jos."

Hunt-Wesson has not been the only company to find itself in such a humorous position. A U.S. airline that proudly advertised swank "rendezvous lounges" available on its Boeing 747 jets may have wished that its promotion had never reached Brazil. After advertising these accommodations, the company belatedly learned that "rendez-vous" in Portuguese represents a room that is rented out for prostitution. Although the promotion was successful in attracting attention, sales were not boosted. No Brazilian wanted to be seen getting on or off the airline's plane. Here again the failure to consider all of the meanings and implications of the translated message was responsible for the subsequent difficulties.

Drawing by Stephen Foster

The above cartoon was used to illustrate the "rendezvous lounges" problem when the author was on the "Today Show" to discuss international business problems.

Several major tobacco companies have also experienced the pitfalls of double meanings. These firms advertised "low-tar" cigarettes in Spanish-speaking countries, but misused the word *brea.* "Brea" literally translates to "tar," but it is the type of tar used in paving streets. Who would care to smoke a "low-asphalt" cigarette?

A classic example of a humorous double-meaning translation blunder involves the General Motors Corporation. What the company had intended to convey to its Belgian market was that the car being promoted had a "Body by Fisher." Instead, the phrase was interpreted in Flemish as "Corpse by Fisher." It was the company's appeal that needed translation in this case, not the actual words.[2]

Translated words may often mean about the same thing, but they may not express the same feelings. As an example, "As smooth as a baby's bottom" was incorrectly translated into Japanese to "As smooth as a baby's ass." Translators must be encouraged to convey the intended mood even if this means using alternate wording rather than a literal translation of the original message.

/Sometimes someone in a company simply forgets that words have well-known double meanings. One firm, for example, experienced troubles conducting market research. It requested information on the annual German production of washers. The firm was actually seeking data on washing machines but, instead, received material on the production of flat metal discs (also known as washers). Here the translation problem was not so much with the translated word or the translator but with the original word./

One final example of the troublesome multiple-meaning word involves the banking industry. An American bank was given a 30-day option on the purchase of a Middle Eastern bank. During the final negotiations, an unfortunate buyer proposed in French that the loans be put into an escrow account. The local sellers, quite humiliated and shocked, quickly left the room shouting, "A reserve for cheating? Never!" The misunderstanding stemmed from the word *escrow* which when translated into French means a gyp. Quite upset, the sellers decided to find another interested party willing to purchase the bank.[3]

Translations play a key role in all aspects of international business, and accuracy is of utmost importance. The degree to which a company can be hurt by one faulty translation is great.

IDIOMS

Having discussed not only those errors resulting from careless translation but also those due to multiple meanings, consider now the third type of blunder: those made during the translation of idioms and expressions. Because of the unique aspect of the idiomatic expressions which characterize every language, this area is often the most difficult. The following examples have been chosen as illustrations.

Everyone is familiar with the Pepsi-Cola advertising slogan "Come Alive with Pepsi." When the campaign was reportedly introduced in Germany, the company was forced to revise the ad because it discovered that the German translation of "Come Alive" became "Come out of the grave." And in Asia, the same phrase translated to "Bring your ancestors back from the dead." The intended meaning of this famous slogan was definitely lost somewhere in the translation.[4]

Most firms realize it takes more than a bilingual dictionary to translate commercial messages and their intended meanings. However, a few firms have used the simplest, most literal translations for their promotions and as a result have found themselves promoting something other than what they had thought. An American company, for instance, advertised its product to a Spanish audience exclaiming that anyone who didn't wear its brand of hosiery just "wouldn't have a leg to stand on." But when the copy was translated, the firm actually declared that the wearer would "only have one leg."

Another case of a troublesome literal translation occurred in French-speaking Quebec. The point-of-sale campaign of a laundry soap company stressed the extra strong cleaning powers of the product and how it was the best to use on the especially dirty parts of the wash, "les parts de sale." When the soap sales declined, the company investigated and discovered that this phrase is comparable to the American slang phrase "private parts."

Drawing by Stephen Foster

The above cartoon was used to illustrate the problem experienced with the slogan "come alive with Pepsi" when the author was on the "Today Show" to talk about international business blunders.

The English expression "touch-toe" was responsible for a blunder made by a dental equipment manufacturer. The company featured the "touch-toe" control of its dental chair movement in a published brochure used to advertise its products to the Soviet market. The translator, however, rendered the description of this feature in such a way that the Russians thought the dentist had to be barefooted to operate the equipment. What a unique feature, indeed!

Several other brief examples of mistranslated English idioms or expressions can be cited to illustrate how often these blunders have been made. One European firm certainly missed the point when it translated the expression "out of sight, out of mind" as "invisible things are insane" in Thailand. There is also the story of the phrase "the spirit is willing, but the flesh is weak" being translated to "the liquor is holding out all right, but the meat has spoiled." And consider, finally, a translation of "Schweppes Tonic Water" to the Italian "il water." The copy was speedily dehydrated to "Schweppes Tonica" because "il water" idiomatically indicates a bathroom.

If anything is to be learned from these examples, it is the necessity for caution in the translation and interpretation of the intended messages. Exact wording should not always be translated literally. This can be most appropriately demonstrated by citing 10 idioms used in the United States. If any of these were to be used in Quebec, for example, then the French translation should not be a literal one but should approximate the local phrase or idiom commonly used there. The U.S. version is mentioned first and is followed by the comparable French Canadian expression.

1. "To murder the King's English" should be translated as "to speak French like a Spanish cow."

2. "Nothing to sneeze at" should become "nothing to spit on."

3. "Welcome as a bull in a china shop" should become "welcome as a dog in a bowling alley."

4. "A little birdie told me so" should become "my little finger told it to me."

5. "To be sitting on the fence" should become "to swim between two streams."

6. "I have a hangover" should become "I have a sore hair."

7. "To cry in one's beer" should become "to have the sad wine."

8. "Unable to make head or tail of it" should become "to lose one's Latin."

9. "To make a mountain out of a molehill" should become "to drown in a glass of water."

10. "You can't teach an old dog new tricks" should become "one does not teach an old monkey to make faces."[5]

/It need not be an entire phrase which needs rewording, but only one simple word. What the people of one country take for granted as the only correct word or sound might be totally inappropriate to others. Take, for example, the words used for animal sounds. In reality, an animal makes the same noise in every country, but humans interpret the sound differently from country to country./Therefore:

Translating Can Be Beastly

Every dog may have his day, but whether he has his "bow-wow" depends on the country he lives in and the "language" he speaks. The French pup says "oua oua," but his Japanese counterpart barks out "wan wan"; and in Italy the canine chorus is made up of cries of "bau

bau." Dogs in Spain say "guau-guau," in Korea "mong-mong," "vovvov" in Norway, and "hav hav" if their dog-house is located in Istanbul.

Animals, it seems, speak in dozens of "foreign languages" just like us people; and just like our human languages, sometimes their sounds are similar and sometimes not at all alike.

Cats say "meow" in America, and their Polish cousins sound pretty much the same when they "miau," as do felines in Holland who "miauw," in Yugoslavia who "mijau," in France who "miaou," and you'd think a Siamese kitten had English lessons when you hear him "miew." But you may need a translator to help you pet a pussycat in Sweden or Indonesia, where "cat-ese" comes out as "jama" and "ngéong," or in Japan, where "nyaw" is what you'll hear.

If you're out for a ride, don't be surprised when your foreign-born mount refuses to "neigh" and tells you instead "hi-hi" (France) or "hii" (Spain). Down on the farm, hens don't "cluck" in most other countries, either. Those three French hens who arrived on the third day of Christmas are more likely to be saying "glouk-glouk." Chickens who completed Spanish III will, of course, run around the barnyard with a "cloc-cloc" here and a "cloc-cloc" there.

Naturally, this onomatopoeic phraseology represents what the animal sounds like to the human listener's ear. Clearly, many of us hear things pretty much the same way; but not all of us do. Cows say "moo" to English-speaking peoples and rather the same thing to the French and Spanish, although spelled "meuh" and "muu." So do piggies, who "oink" in America and "groink" on the continent, as do ducks, whose French "coin-coin" or Spanish "cuak-cuak" are not much different from our homegrown "quacks."

Sheep and goats, on the other hand, speak more sharply in French and Spanish than they do in English. The soft "aa" sound of "baa" and "maa" becomes the sharper sound of a stretched long "a" in those languages, as "bé bé," "mé mé," and "bee, mee."

One animal who seems to sound alike to most of the

world except us is the king of the barnyard. Only American roosters wake the family with a "cock-a-doodle-doo." In other parts of the world, dawn is heralded by "cocorico" (France), "kikiriki" (Spain), "cutcurigu" (Romainia), "cuc-cu-cu" (Vietnam), "chicchirichi" (Italy), "kukurikú" (Hungary), "kokoriko" (Turkey), or "kykeliky" (Norway).[6]

Obviously, companies which sell pet food and supplies and those taking the risky approach of featuring animals in promotions need to take extra precautions when speaking for these animals. If the messages are to be effective, then the firms must be sure that they are communicating in languages that can be understood.

LESSONS TO BE LEARNED

A firm is not totally helpless when trying to avoid translation blunders. There are several methods known which can help a company avert potential disasters.

Use of local people

A company may hire an exceptionally brilliant translator, but certain types of errors can still easily crop up. Even though the individual may have an extraordinary gift for the language or have studied in the country, idiomatic expressions and slang may be unfamiliar to him. Therefore, in many cases, it is a wise decision to also hire a local translator, one familiar with the local slang and unusual idioms, to "backtranslate."

Backtranslation

One of the best techniques available to aid in the reduction of translation errors is known as "backtranslation." The principle underlying backtranslation requires that one individual translate the message into the desired foreign language and that another party translate the foreign version back to the original language. This allows one to determine if the intended message is the one actually being presented.

An Australian soft drink company discovered the value of backtranslation during the planning stages of its Hong Kong market entry. The company had hoped to introduce its successful slogan "Baby, it's cold inside," but before advertising with the translated version of the slogan, the firm had it translated back into English. This proved to be a wise decision. The message backtranslated to "Small mosquito, on the inside it is very cold." Even though "small mosquito" was a local colloquial expression for a small child, the phrase simply did not convey the same thing as the friendly English slang word *baby* for *woman*. The intended message would have been lost had the original translated version been used.

Backtranslation reveals many translation errors, but it can prove frustrating if done by mediocre translators. Naturally, the better the translator, the fewer the problems and delays. The difficulty, therefore, lies in the determination of the ability of a potential translator. One slow and expensive method to determine this ability is to allow the translator a trial run. This will indicate any problems, but it then becomes necessary to determine if the errors were committed by the original translator or by the person translating back to the first language.

Selection of a translator

\Firms requiring major or important translation work should thoroughly investigate the possible translator and company./The following points should be covered in the interview.

1. Does the translator maintain or have access to a library or reference books dealing with the appropriate subject and industry?

2. Does the translator understand the required technical terms? Does he or she know of the foreign words for these specialized terms? If not, how does he or she intend to learn them?

3. Does the translator have a staff or access to experts in various fields (i.e., law)?

4. Will someone check the work? If so, what are the credentials of the assistant? (It is often advisable to request references and copies of material translated for other clients.)

5. How recently has the translator been to the country? (Sometimes it is necessary to determine just how current the translator's knowledge is. Because languages do change, it is not just enough to have someone familiar with the foreign language and culture. Even a native tends to lose track of slang and idioms after being away from home for a few years. Ten-year-old experience may prove to be too old.)

Helping the translator

Once a translator has been chosen, there are several things a company can do to ease the job. For instance, since it has often taken the company several months to develop good promotional materials, a translator should not be asked to translate the material overnight. Given adequate time, a much better translation is likely to result. Simple literal translation is not generally appropriate, so a translator needs time to be creative.

This is not to say that the translator should not be given a deadline. It is important to tell the person when the material must be finished and its expected promotion time. On occasion, a manager has failed to mention the season, and the translator has assumed an inappropriate time. A company does little to enhance its image when it runs a winter advertisement in the summer. (A few companies have also blundered by advertising during inappropriate seasons when they forgot that the Southern Hemisphere has the opposite seasons of the Northern Hemisphere.)

Naturally, it is important for the translator to understand the type of media to be used and the general characteristics of the audience. This allows the person to determine the proper level of formality and the correct tone. A translator must be given the freedom to modify original wording, since exact literal translations can prove disastrous.

If possible, firms are advised to reduce the use of overly technical terms and to avoid industry jargon. It is also advisable to limit the use of large numbers. Any number over 10,000 may be easily mistranslated. The number "billion," for example, numerically contains 9 zeroes in the United States, but contains 12 zeroes in Europe.

Since humor is almost impossible to translate, it is best to avoid jokes in advertising. What is deemed funny by some is often not considered humorous by others.

Also, because the translated version of a message

may require more words than the original, it is not wise to limit the translator to a particular amount of time or space. Doing so may seriously jeopardize the effectiveness of the message.

Finally, a translator should be provided with as much relevant information as possible. The translator should be informed of the message's objectives and what is essential to the theme. By allowing him to examine previous company translations as well as translated slogans of competing companies, he can not only assure that any key phrase associated with the company is included but can avoid accidentally using any competitor's phrases.

Using English in non-English-speaking countries

Sometimes companies have found that the best solution to the translation problem is simply to not translate the material. If the locals can understand English or if they simply don't need to comprehend the message, then it may be safer for a firm from an English-speaking country to stick with the English copy. The use of translators is always risky because they are putting words into the corporate mouth. A firm does not need for them to put a foot in there also.

To reduce problems which may occur when English is used in a non-English-speaking country:

1. Keep the entire message short and simple, including the words and sentences.
2. Avoid jargon or slang.
3. Avoid idioms.
4. Avoid humor, if possible.
5. Use appropriate currencies and measurements.

6. Cite examples, if feasible.

7. Repeat important points.

If the advertisement is a verbal one, the English speaker should:

1. Speak slowly.

2. Speak carefully and pronounce all words correctly.

3. Pause between sentences.

Sometimes it is best to not even use English. To reduce translation needs and overcome communication difficulties in countries experiencing high levels of illiteracy, visual methods of communication are sometimes used. Libby, for instance, has successfully promoted its products through inexpensive commercials featuring a clown enjoying Libby products. In these ads, no words are spoken.

As it is very likely that during some part of the overseas planning or management someone from the company will engage in a conversation in English with an individual who has some difficulty understanding English, the following guidelines should be considered:

1. Time should be allowed for questions and discussion.

2. Patience is important—permit the individual to find the words to respond.

3. Questions should be asked to determine if the message has been comprehended.

4. The individual should be complimented and reassured of his or her ability to speak English.

5. Express gratefulness that the individual is speaking English.

6. Express regret that the conversation could not have been spoken in the other person's language.

(It should be noted, however, that speaking a few polite, social words in the other language is always useful and is highly recommended.)

Ideally, company literature and material should be provided prior to the conversation. This allows the other individual a chance to prepare and should greatly increase his comprehension. After the discussion, sending a summary to the person should also increase the likelihood that the conversation was correctly understood.

During World War II, the phrase "loose lips sink ships" was used to discourage people from talking about military matters when they were within the hearing range of strangers. For international business people, the phrase might be modified to "misunderstood lips sink corporations." Multinational corporations will encounter enough unavoidable and unpredictable problems to be tried and tested. They need not make avoidable blunders as well.

SUMMARY

Faulty translations have caused more blunders than any other error committed in international business. These translation mistakes have destroyed promotions, negotiations, and numerous other aspects of a company's day-to-day operations. However, through the use of local input, backtranslation, and proper selection and treatment of translators, these blunders are avoidable.

6 STRATEGY

Over the years, companies have committed a wide variety of strategic errors. Supply decisions have created troubles for some companies while other firms have experienced difficulties through their choices of overseas partners. In a few cases, blunders were caused by "simple" pricing mistakes. Others have involved complex strategies in which several inappropriate decisions were made. These and other strategic blunders will be discussed in this chapter.

SUPPLY PROBLEMS

Most companies try to save money by purchasing supplies in large quantities. There are, however, logical limits governing this strategy. One example of excessive supply purchasing occurred in Chile. Until recently, the Chilean government levied high tariffs on automobile imports. Over time, this created a large, pent-up demand for cars. In the late 1970s the government began to reduce tariffs radically and, consequently, demand quickly outstripped supply. By 1981, these tariffs had dropped so low that large numbers of Chileans could afford new autos. Because dealers were unable to fill the vast number of orders, a five-month waiting period for most automobile models was not unusual. Believing that this demand might be unlimited, dealers ordered up to 10 times their normal number of cars for 1982 even though the economy began experiencing a recession and the new models were higher priced. A flooded market resulted. Most of the demand for autos had already been satisfied, and few of the fairly new cars needed to be replaced. Economic uncertainty and higher prices also kept customers away. The result was that inventories grew so high that dealers had no room to store the cars. Many loads (more than a year's supply) were left on board ships lying offshore, incurring high storage costs. The lesson: Optimistic, straight-line projections of sales figures are obviously dangerous. Temporary causes of demand should be analyzed and estimates made to determine the amount of pent-up demand still remaining.

Nigeria, though, probably experienced the largest purchasing blunder. Due to increased oil revenues that resulted from the sharp rise of oil prices in the mid 1970s, Nigeria began to initiate major modernization programs. An economically minded bureaucrat decided to purchase the total amount of cement needed to construct all of the new building being planned. Because Nigeria did not have its own cement plant, the cement was ordered from other countries. Soon it began to arrive by the shipload. The dock workers were unable to unload the cement as fast as it arrived, so the ships were forced to await their turn for unloading. Within weeks, there were so many shiploads of unloaded cement that someone computed the length of time required to unload all of the ships. Even with an expanded dock in Lagos, it was discovered that the 20 million tons of cement could not be fully unloaded for 40 years! Much of the cement had to be dumped overboard; the cost to hold the ships until unloading was greater than the cost of re-ordering the cement.[1]

EverReady, Ltd., of England encountered supply problems of a different nature. Hoping to introduce its product to the Nigerians, the company chose a strategy which stressed broad market penetration. The EverReady name and battery were heavily promoted, and a large production run was shipped to Lagos. No problems occurred during the unloading, but the firm probably wished that some had. Apparently a defective chemical had been used during the production of the batteries, and those shipped to Lagos were worthless. Unfortunately, someone had forgotten to test them prior to shipment. Although the first batteries appearing on the heavily promoted Nigerian market sold quickly, word soon spread that the product was not dependable. Since no backup supply of good batteries was available, the promotional effort was wasted, and the firm developed a reputation in Nigeria as being an unreliable company which produced poor goods. Later, when normal batteries reached the Nigerian market, consumers avoided them. It took years for EverReady to overcome its initial reputation there.

Large department stores often purchase stock from many sources, including foreign countries. It is especially important for the buyers of these goods to be familiar with local foreign customs. They should also be fluent in the required language or have translation assistance. One over-confident buyer created quite a problem for her Italian firm. Believing that she knew English fairly well, she was sent to Britain to purchase clothing. When she found some appropriate sweaters at Bourne and Hollingsworth, she attempted to request "four to five thousand pounds worth." It became quite obvious, however, that there had been a "misunderstanding" when she returned to Italy and the delivery trucks began arriving. They were carrying the "forty-five" thousand pounds worth ($90,000 U.S.) that she had actually ordered!

Often a company is initially successful overseas but later experiences major difficulties. This occurred to one company which located in Africa. The firm began purchasing huge supplies of old, used inner tubes discarded by the U.S. Army during World War II. These inexpensive discards were easily cut to form rubber bands, and soon the company had captured the entire local rubber band market. After making over $1 million on the venture, the owners felt extremely successful and clever until someone pointed out that the supply of old inner tubes had dried up. The war was over, the army had left, and the newer tires of the few vehicles still in use were tubeless. Awash with money and confidence, the managers decided to "go big league" and buy modern equipment. The machinery and supplies, of course, were expensive and quite difficult to maintain. The company, failing to realize how different the new system would be, had no particular abilities in the "new" process and was unable to produce at affordable prices. The strategy failed, and all of the former profits were lost.

Supply difficulties have hindered a number of companies. As was mentioned in the first chapter, one U.S. pineapple firm was unable to transport its fruit down the river to its processing plant because it had failed to analyze the typical river conditions. Similarly, the Soviet Union built a large, expensive steel mill for India only to discover that the mill had been located in an area without adequate transportation facilities. The steel mill, intended as a showplace for

Soviet propaganda purposes, turned out to be an embarrassment instead.

The Hanna Mining Company reportedly experienced some logistical problems in Brazil. One of the firm's basic strategies involved its ability to supply extract ore at increasing rates over time. Since a small-scale operation would not prove profitable, the company decided that if it could expand every year it would become a profitable operation by the time the firm was able to export 2 million tons of ore. Few initial problems developed. The company, however, was unable to expand its operations as expected because local transportation facilities were inadequate In this case, the firm's initial strategy failed because it had no way to transport the ore to market even though it maintained the capability to extract the required ore. (It should be noted that Hanna Mining reports that this was not a foreseeable problem since the local railroad authorities failed to fulfill the contract's maximum delivery requirement.)

Another firm developed problems when it tried to buy steel plates from Japanese manufacturers. At the root of this blunder was the company's failure to understand the Japanese tendency to answer "yes." By inviting all of the Japanese plate producers to bid, the company felt that it would attain the lowest prices. The low bidder offered to sell at such an appealing price that the firm decided to order all of the needed galvanized steel plates from that particular Japanese company. The Japanese firm was first contacted, however, to assure product availability because the quantity required was so large. "Yes" the company responded; it would fill the large order. The U.S. corporation confidently awaited the shipment. Eventually a small, partial shipment arrived containing plates which had obviously been hand dipped. Since during the normal production process, machines do all of the dipping, the U.S. firm became suspicious. Upon visiting the Japanese plant, its suspicions were confirmed. The plant was quite small and simply could not supply the necessary quantities. Although the Japanese managers knew this would be the case, they did not want to lose face by admitting that their company was so small. They had simply hoped that all would be worked out.

CHOOSING A PARTNER

It might seem that the creation of a joint venture would prevent all of the problems encountered by a company "going overseas." With the combined expertise and efforts of both local and foreign firms, major problems or possible blunders would surely be eliminated. However, although certain types of errors are definitely less likely, a multitude of other problems can arise and pose a serious threat to the venture's success.

More than a few firms have discovered their joint ventures were not as problem-free as expected. For example, one U.S. firm that entered into a joint venture with some South American capitalists did not fully comprehend its initial errors until some five years later. At the time of the company's commitment, its South American partners were in favor with those in the local government. However, the joint venture began to gradually experience various forms of host government harrassment and, consequently, profits slowly declined. Investment money, effort, and time were lost by the U.S. partner. What had happened? The U.S. company had failed to analyze the situation thoroughly. Early analyses should have revealed the existence of a volatile political scene and the degree of political involvement in local business practices.

A company should create a joint venture only after giving the idea careful consideration. Although another firm may be "willing and waiting," this does not necessarily assure success. One U.S. manager found this to be especially true. During an inspection of the company's European operations, he also met with a number of Belgian pump manufacturing executives. Because one particular company exhibited a great deal of interest in forming a partnership, a joint enterprise was quickly formed. A person from Belgium was established as the president of the new company, and the U.S. firm's manager in Belgium became the vice president for manufacturing and engineering. However, friction between these two men and company losses precipitated a crisis. The partnership was dissolved, and the U.S. company bought up all of the Belgian shares at book value. The result: It was many years before the operation became profitable. Undoubtedly, the U.S. firm's unfortunate choice of a partner hindered this venture's success. Partners must be selected with caution, and personalities should be considered.

In 1945, W. R. Grace and Company and a Colombian firm, the Pinturas Colombianas, formed a joint venture. Not long after the creation of this paint-manufacturing partnership, conflict arose partially as a result of the competitive outlets each firm operated independently for the distribution of the paint. Approximately 10 years after the venture's formation, Grace and Company was forced to sell its shares to the Colombian partner. Inevitable sources of conflict should not be overlooked during the initial planning stages of a partnership.

Although blunders are often caused by a company's failure to thoroughly investigate potential partners, sometimes a firm's failure to take advantage of a possible joint venture or licensing agreement also results in losses. For instance, shortly after World War II, parts "specifically for use in" equipment manufactured by the Caterpillar Tractor Company began surfacing for sale in various markets. These products had neither been approved nor manufactured by the Caterpillar Company. The firm, however, was unable to establish any legal claims. If the company had initially sought out a local partner, the demand for these similar parts most assuredly would have benefited Caterpillar. As it turned out, the local manufacturers of the parts saw no reason to avoid competing with the totally foreign-owned Caterpillar Tractor Company.

Licensing decisions are as difficult to analyze as those decisions involving the creation of a joint venture. Failure to make the correct decision at the right time can result in the loss of substantial long-range business prospects and potential profits. In one case, a U.S. manufacturer not only licensed the manufacture and sale of its products to an English firm but also granted the firm the exclusive right to sublicense the U.S. expertise to other countries. At the time the decision was made, the company was not interested in expanding overseas. The firm believed that it was best to simply collect the royalties and thus eliminate the need to provide additional investment money. Within a few years, worldwide markets for the firm's products developed. Naturally, the company greatly regretted its earlier decision permitting exclusive licensing.

A similar situation involved a U.S. pharmaceutical firm which licensed its manufacturing techniques to an Asian company. The Asian company, heavily promoting the products, enjoyed great success. As a result of the licensing terms, however, almost all of the tremendous profits were reaped by the Asian company. Having never realized the product's potential, the U.S. company had permitted the licensing. If the U.S. firm had committed to a more direct form of involvement, such as equity participation, it could have earned greater profits. In this instance, the company's failure to carefully study the market and product opportunities eventually resulted in its loss of profits.

Sometimes the licensee, although pleased to have been granted the license, is not as enthusiastic about the product as the licensor. One U.S. firm discovered this when it granted an exclusive license to a Japanese company. The Japanese company was given the right to manufacture and sell one of the U.S. firm's specialty products for a period of 20 years. Market studies had indicated that the product, which had been extremely successful in the United States, was destined to replace some of the more conventional materials currently in use in Japan. The U.S. firm had carefully studied its potential licensees and had chosen the Japanese company because of its strength of distribution, size, and record of profit performance. However, the Japanese firm, continuing to push the more conventional materials, failed to promote the new product actively. Since the contract included no agreement concerning minimum royalties, the U.S.

company earned no income for the first 10 years. Having failed to recognize the Japanese company's marketing initiatives and lack of interest, the U.S. firm was forced to accept the fact that it could not enter the market itself until the expiration of the 20-year license.

Many other firms have also suffered because of lack of foresight. Consider the U.S. company that manufactured military equipment during World War II. Having failed to engage in product modification or to establish service facilities, the company's highly regarded reputation began to diminish when the war ended. To reestablish its prior position, it hurriedly agreed to a licensing arrangement with a European manufacturer. The agreement permitted the exchange and sharing of information, design, and product development. Not long after the commitment had been made, European opportunities arose encouraging the manufacture of similar products. However, because of the license agreement, the U.S. firm was essentially excluded from any direct participation in the European market. The European licensee reaped the substantial profits and, being exposed to the expertise of the U.S. company, even became the U.S. company's main European competitor.

The natural tendency for any company is to "get in while the going is good." One U.S. firm particularly eager to begin operations in India quickly negotiated terms and completed arrangements with its local partners. Certain required documents, however, such as the industrial license, foreign collaboration agreements, capital issues permit, import licenses for machinery and equipment, etc., were slow in being issued. Trying to expedite governmental approval of these items, the U.S. firm agreed to accept a lower royalty fee than originally stipulated. Despite all of this extra effort, the project was not greatly expedited, and the lower royalty fee reduced the firm's profit by approximately half of a million dollars over the life of the agreement.

As the economic importance of Japan has grown, so have companies' desires to market products there. Entering the Japanese market can prove quite difficult, though, due to unique cultural and social norms. An executive from Lucerne, Switzerland, negotiating a business venture with a Japanese firm, for example, failed to recognize the role personal sentiment played in Japanese business behavior and paid the penalty. The president of the Japanese company sponsored a party in Tokyo and exclaimed, "I will not do business with a man who does not like us!" The Lucerne executive thought he had concealed his dislike for the Japanese during his stay, but the president of the Japanese company had seen through his mask. The Japanese executive, therefore, refused to proceed with the business deal even though the partnership would undoubtedly have proven mutually profitable.

Heinz also experienced difficulties in the Japanese market. Attempting to enter the market quickly, Heinz gained a minority interest in a company called Nichiro Fisheries. Not only did the fishery name imply that all of the products were fish oriented but the partnership was not appropriate. Nichiro Fisheries simply did not hold enough capital or maintain the broad distribution channels required by Heinz to market its products adequately.

Failing to consider the moral values or reliability of a possible partner can also prove disastrous. In some countries, it is normal for a company to take whatever it can from its partner. When both parties expect this, reasonable safeguards can be developed. When one company is not aware of this practice, though, blunders can certainly result. For example, after being visited by overseas managers, a U.S. chemical manufacturer agreed to a partnership. The strategy developed involved the export of raw materials by the U.S. firm and the manufacture of products by the foreign company. All of the details were carefully stipulated in a contract, but within six months of the first large shipment of raw materials, the partnership broke up. What had gone wrong? Credit terms had not been met, earnings were disputed, and payments had not been sent. The well-known and "respected" local partner had gained part of his visibility, however, through his ability to delay or avoid paying his obligations—a common local practice. The U.S. company should have been aware of this local system. It then would have known to require payment in advance (the locally accepted practice) or could have established some other financially safe arrangement. To the local courts, the U.S. firm appeared foolish and deserved the loss—after all, the company had failed to follow good, normal, business practices.[2]

PRICING

Setting an appropriate price for a product is often much more difficult than it appears. If only one insignificant detail of the pricing procedure is overlooked or misjudged, major troubles can develop for the firm.

Consider the experience of a company trying to market cans of luncheon meat. In order to beat the prices of its competitors, the firm slightly cut its prices by rounding them off to easy-to-record, even numbers. The customary prices of the competitors' products were a bit higher, and to the disappointment of the company, customers seemed quite willing to pay the minor extra charge. A local business practice was actually involved in this mishap. Local retail outlets usually operated on very small profit margins. These retailers found their customers would not request the small change due when purchasing the fractionally higher priced cans of meat. Naturally, in order to keep their "tip," the retailers heavily promoted the competition. It took the firm over six months to readjust its price and begin selling its product again.

Sometimes the price set is simply too high. In the 1960s, for example, an American food company attempted to sell its soup at a price of 80 cents per can. Because most French housewives considered soup to be a minor appetizer, they were unwilling to spend the required amount of money, and consequently, the soup did not sell well. The Delacre line of luxury biscuits promoted under the Pepperidge Farm label encountered similar problems when it was introduced into the United States. The biscuits did not sell well until the British firm Peek Freanline introduced them at a much lower price. Products are not prized in all countries, so what some may be willing to pay highly for, others may not. In a foreign environment, any assumption concerning a product's "special value" is dangerous. Unless the market is clearly established, the implementation of a high pricing strategy is not likely to achieve high sales volumes.

In the early 1960s, Princess Housewares experienced pricing difficulties in the German marketplace. During that period in Germany, small appliances were generally distributed to retail outlets through independent wholesalers, but department stores, mail order houses, and discount outlets were gaining popularity. Due to their size, these large retailers were able to obtain products at lower prices and could market goods at very competitive prices. Consequently, resale price maintenance became very difficult. In order to protect the small retailers' margins, however, Princess Housewares decided to enforce undiscounted prices. Thus, the company eventually found itself at a competitive disadvantage when selling to the large retailers and was greatly hurt by its failure to accept this new up-and-coming retail trend. Similar marketing trends in the United States a few years earlier should have signaled the increasing importance of large retail outlets.

Price negotiation can also prove to be a tricky undertaking. If the company negotiators are unaware of local customs, inappropriate prices are quite likely to result. This risk is best illustrated by examining the negotiation process involving Americans and Japanese. American managers are accustomed to pressured decision making and are often given the authority to make final decisions. Japanese managers, on the other hand, prefer to negotiate more slowly, tend to make decisions by group consensus, and always politely listen to everyone in their group before reaching an official decision. Because Americans are generally unaware of these tendencies, they have often created problems for themselves. A typical situation involves an American negotiating with Japanese managers in order to buy or sell some product or service. The American, often anxious to complete the deal, tends (in the eyes of the Japanese) to rush the negotiation process. All too often, when the time for price discussion arrives, the American will quickly suggest a price.

Being used to the give-and-take of negotiating, the American usually does not make the best possible offer at the start nor necessarily expect it to be accepted. Here is where the troubles arise. When people hesitate, an American tends to assume that the price mentioned is an unacceptable one. Therefore, he will sometimes hastily improve the offer even before it is rejected or the process is unsuccessfully terminated. But the American negotiating with Japanese managers may commit a blunder by quickly altering the price. This has happened on numerous occasions, but in at least one reported case, an American raised the price he was willing to pay three times after the Japanese were prepared to accept. Unaware of Japanese customs, he did not realize that the hesitation and discussion between the Japanese (in Japanese, of course) were not a result of unhappiness over the price quoted. With each higher price offer, the Japanese negotiators expressed amazement (in Japanese) but then proceeded to check out their colleagues' opinions. This delay only unwittingly encouraged the American to offer even more.

Many companies have been able to buy or sell merchandise at the right price but have stated the prices in wrong currencies. Because totally accurate exchange-rate forecasting is not possible, some mistakes have been made. The direction of currency movement is fairly predictable, though, and should be considered when a company prices a contract for future payment.

Similarly, in most countries, inflation is fairly predictable. The failure to analyze inflationary factors has hurt a number of companies. A German company, for example, agreed to a $163 million Algerian construction contract. The price set was fair enough at the time of the commitment, but costs rose dramatically during the life of the contract. Unfortunately, the firm had failed to include protective price escalators in the original contract. Additionally, it soon discovered that payments were made in the local Algerian currency which had also declined in value. This double-edged sword cut out all of the company's expected profits and cost the firm millions of dollars.

Credit, another price-related variable, is often critical to the marketing strategy. Although the product might be appropriately priced, it may not sell if credit terms are unacceptable. Consider a multinational firm that had carefully test marketed its specially modified washing machines and concluded that they would sell well in Latin America. Sales were slow even though a large shipment had been made available. Eventually the firm discovered the trouble: local competitors were making their sales on credit. Apparently those participating in the market test had assumed that credit would be made available since it was the local business practice. So, when asked during the test if they would buy, they replied "yes." Only after they discovered that no credit would be provided did they change their minds and decide not to purchase the product. As evidenced, all aspects of pricing and selling strategies must be considered carefully.

COMPLEX PROBLEMS

Although some of the strategic errors committed by multinational corporations are fairly easy to understand, others are complex and involve several components. Simmons, Ford, Raytheon, Imperial-Eastman, and General Electric have all experienced complex problems within their foreign operations.

The Simmons Co., a marketer of quality beds, might never have taken the plunge to expand to Japan if it had known the magnitude of the problems it would encounter. With numerous successful overseas ventures under its belt and confident of its product, the Simmons Co. set out in the early 1960s to manufacture mattresses in Japan. Four years later, the company was still experiencing substantial losses in Japan. Several complex problems plagued its operation. Although aware of many of the difficulties surrounding the Japanese market, the company had underestimated the degree of complexity present in the Japanese environment.

Simmons had realized that it would face several obstacles. Not only did most Japanese still sleep on futons (a type of floor mat) but the company also recognized that the complex and unusual Japanese distribution system could be quite confusing. The fact that an oligopolistic group of local manufacturers vied for control of the limited market only complicated matters further.

However, because the firm strongly believed in its product and know-how, Simmons Tokyo (later, Simmons, Japan) was organized in October 1964. Entry into the market had been timed to coincide with the Tokyo Olympic Games when the demand for beds would sharply rise over a short period of time. Early production progressed smoothly, but problems developed later.

Among the difficulties the company encountered was its choice of a sales force. Because of the existence of social-class differences and subtle language styles, the salesmen were most effective only if they and the client were of the same class. Therefore, the initial eight-man sales force had to be rigorously screened. Even after an appropriate personnel choice, a problem ensued. None of the salesmen had ever slept on a bed! How could they be expected to sincerely endorse Simmons's product?

Simmons also learned that it had overpriced its beds by as much as $60 above domestic prices. Even the distribution system proved baffling—everyday conduct and favors were often intertwined. A customer might engage in business with a supplier to whom he owed a favor regardless of the price difference, thus producing a tangled distribution network with complex relationships. Since no Japanese wished to lose face, Simmons also discovered that trying to operate outside of this established system was quite difficult.

And finally, Simmons also made an unfortunate decision regarding advertising media. The company chose print media and concentrated its distribution in the Tokyo area instead of using television, the most effective and penetrating advertising medium in Japan.[3]

Another U.S. firm encountered different problems in its efforts to "go international." An electronics firm was approached by a foreign firm interested in creating a joint venture in Asia. Because the product potential appeared so high, the company wished to establish the venture fully before any competition could be enticed into the market. So an agreement was quickly arranged. In its haste, however, the U.S. firm failed to investigate fully such important marketing factors as competitive environment, market maturity, distribution requirements, marketing costs, penetration strategy, promotional programs, etc. Also, the U.S. company did not carefully evaluate its partner's experience, general know-how, and operational procedures. As a result, problems that should have been considered and resolved during the initial planning stages of the venture were still cropping up years later.

Ford Motor Company has established a very successful record in international business. In fact, it has been the most successful U.S. automotive company engaging in business outside of North America. Even Ford, however, has encountered its share of troubles. In 1973, for instance, after experiencing a major success in the Philippines with the Fiera, Ford introduced the vehicle in Thailand. But it sold poorly. Ford had overestimated its reputation and had incorrectly assumed that Thai consumers would prefer a Ford to other cars. The company had also assumed that the Fiera's low price would attract customers, but it was not prepared to offer the credit terms available through its competitors. Furthermore, the Fiera frequently experienced breakdowns because vehicles in Thailand were usually overloaded two or three times beyond normally designed capacities. By the time a sturdier model was introduced, the Fiera had already earned a reputation for being unreliable.

When Raytheon's local partner withdrew from its Sicilian joint venture, EISI, due to declining profits, Raytheon was unable to find a replacement partner for its television tube producing plant. The plant needed to be modernized, but such alterations required substantial capital investment. So Raytheon tried to continue selling the out-of-date tubes. Not only were the tubes outdated but the market was saturated. Even though sales dropped significantly in Italy, the company failed to develop any export markets. Losses continued to mount, so the firm fired one fourth of its employees. The firing of Sicilian employees without prior governmental approval and major payments to the employees involved, however, was an extremely unacceptable business practice. The result: The local governmental officials took control of the plant, and Raytheon lost over $25 million.[4]

In a different part of Europe, another large U.S. corporation came very close to committing a similar error. To realize substantial cost savings, the company planned a massive cost-reduction program which involved the layoff of a significant number of employees. It was fortunate for the company that prior to the initiation of the program it learned that layoffs based on these grounds were highly unacceptable in the host country. Since much of the firm's business involved agencies of the host government, this action surely would have evoked great unhappiness and the government agencies would have been pressured to place their orders with other suppliers. Sales undoubtedly would have dropped, but even more damaging and far-reaching would have been the company's loss of reputation. Indeed the blunder was avoided, but the company had needlessly allocated time and money to develop a plan that never could have worked. Much waste could have been eliminated had the corporation been aware of the local business practice.

Imperial-Eastman Corporation encountered numerous problems in the operations of its various overseas enterprises. In at least one instance, the company experienced unexpected difficulties when it failed to retain its overseas U.S. personnel for a long enough period of time. Before the operation's critical start-up period was completely past, the company relieved its U.S. personnel and relied solely on its locally hired staff to continue running the operation. However, as critical problems developed, Imperial-Eastman discovered that the local staff was not sufficiently experienced to handle the difficult problems resulting from the new operation. In other ventures, the company suffered from poor estimates of initial inventory needs which created production delivery disruptions. Losses were incurred when the firm did not allow for delayed delivery and subcontractors failed to deliver on time.[5]

A precarious balance seems to exist between the number of foreign managers needed and the number of U.S. managers needed for a successful operation. Imperial-Eastman experienced problems by relying too heavily on inexperienced local managers, but General Electric encountered troubles by its placement and retention of U.S. employees in most managerial positions. In some cases, because the U.S. employees were unfamiliar with the local business practices, they unknowingly nullified the firm's ability to compete with local business people. G.E. also experienced other overseas troubles. Some of its foreign ventures were viewed initially with so much optimism and enthusiasm that the original projections and timetables were unrealistic and consequently led to disappointment. Because of these early letdowns, management tended to be wary of complete ownership or majority interest in its overseas operations. Furthermore, the company tried for too long to maintain the distribution channels it had developed through years of effort in South America. By doing so, it became particularly vulnerable to the rise of innovative competition during a period of rapidly changing environments and thus failed to aggressively seek out and adopt new methods of distribution.[6]

ADDITIONAL MISTAKES IN STRATEGY

Sometimes a company finds that its golden touch is not golden everywhere. The Tengelmann group of West Germany discovered this when it bought an American supermarket chain, the A&P. The firm's normal strategy of offering a limited line of low-cost, store-brand groceries worked well for Tengelmann in Europe. However, its attempts to use this same strategy in the United States failed and resulted in a $75 million loss over a two-year period. As the new chairman, James Wood, admitted, "The mistake we foreigners often make is to judge the U.S. on the basis of what we know about Europe. Americans want a fuller range of products from a supermarket than people on the other side of the water."[7]

Europeans, of course, are not the only ones who sometimes assume that what works at home will also work abroad. A highly successful American supermarket chain experienced difficulties in its overseas venture also. The American company and a renowned Japanese company, Sumitomo Shoji Kaisha, Ltd., formed a supermarket joint venture in Japan. Small Japanese retailers, however, strongly objected to the bond created by these two giants, so Sumitomo Shoji helped set up a dummy company and permitted the U.S. firm to manage it. The U.S. company employed the techniques proven successful in U.S. supermarket management but could not produce profitable financial statements in Japan. After studying the Japanese distribution system, the Japanese traditional ways of doing business, and the characteristics of the Japanese customers, the U.S. management decided that it was necessary to convert the operations to a "Japanese mode." The Japanese customers found the new system acceptable, and the venture began to thrive.

Many cases can be cited to illustrate the importance of a thorough preliminary market study. As one example, consider the U.S. company that discovered that its lack of understanding of its Japanese partner's distribution network greatly hindered the venture's success. Hoping to achieve optimum market penetration for its product, which was relatively new to the Japanese, the U.S. firm selected the best distribution networks of its Japanese partner and set up a single-level system of wholesalers. Even though the product sold well through the channels where distribution was achieved, market penetration fell short of expectation because the needed national coverage was not available. Although the original decision to use the partner's best distribution networks appeared wise, the firm had failed to realize fully how numerous and diffuse the Japanese retail outlet networks can be and overestimated the effectiveness of its planned network.

Distribution problems do not only occur within the Japanese system. A major U.S. manufacturer of mixed feed for poultry, for example, decided to establish a market in Spain after it had received encouraging results from a preliminary market study. Although local business people advised the firm against forming a subsidiary that was wholly owned, the company went ahead with its plans. A factory was built, a technical staff was brought in, and operations were set up. However, once production began, the firm discovered that it could not sell its products.

Why? The Spanish poultry growers and feed producers comprised a closely knit family, and newcomers were not welcome. So to overcome this obstacle, the firm bought a series of chicken farms. To its dismay, the company discovered that no one would buy its chickens either! Had the company heeded the local advice and understood the local business practices, these difficulties could have been avoided.

Many other companies have suffered from similar pitfalls. For instance, one American cosmetics manufacturer experienced difficulties when it tried to market its products in France solely through a chain store. By utilizing this method, the firm felt it could achieve maximum market exposure while holding down marketing and distribution costs. In some countries, this system might have worked. In France, however, "perfumers" (small local retailers specializing in cosmetics), are traditionally considered the opinion makers, and most manufacturers give exclusive franchise to two or three local perfumers. Word-of-mouth promotion is vital, and the public relies heavily on the opinions of these perfumers. When it bypassed them, the American company angered the perfumers to the point that they discredited the American product and damaged the manufacturer's reputation in France.

Companies have experienced a great many difficulties as a result of poor strategy decisions. As an illustration, consider the aerospace division of Ling-Temco-Vought (LTV) which tried to develop a mechanical substitute for the water buffalo. Because the company's research and development facilities were located in the United States, the firm tried to develop the machine in the United States. Unfortunately, this was not a wise decision. The machines created by the company were eventually exposed to the unique Asian weather conditions and developed various problems.

Host governmental approval is an extremely important variable involved in the determination of a company's overseas success. Massey-Ferguson learned this when it reportedly experienced some difficulties after it entered into a 51 percent ownership venture in Turkey to produce tractors. A large-scale plan was developed that permitted an initial annual production capacity of 50,000 engines and called for the later addition of a second facility that would produce another 30,000 tractors a year. The company's high hopes were never realized. Massey-Ferguson reportedly failed to investigate thoroughly the implications of the economic and political pressures present in Turkey and the stability of the government. To assure its market success, the company needed strong governmental backing. This support never fully materialized (a result which some claim could have been predicted), and the venture was formally terminated in 1970.[8]

The U.S. lock manufacturer, Yale and Towne, can attest to the desirability of gaining not only local governmental support but also the acceptance of local competitors. In the 1960s, in order to gain entry into the Japanese market, Yale and Towne planned to form a joint venture with Copal Co., Ltd., a local Japanese camera shutter manufacturer. The plans were quite ambitious and included a projected annual production target of 600,000 units or 20 percent of the Japanese market. Local manufacturers, threatened by these plans, petitioned the Japanese Ministry of

International Trade and Industry requesting the prevention of this investment. Not surprisingly, Yale and Towne experienced a delay in the processing of its application. By April 1965, the local lock industry was included in a list of industries that fell under the Law for Acceleration of Modernization of Small Enterprise (a section of the 1950 Foreign Investment Law). The industry, therefore, gained special protection and development incentives from the government. Eventually the Yale and Towne application was rejected. Had the company initially shown more discretion, the local manufacturers may have accepted the new competition without pursuing governmental protection.

In another case, a U.S. consumer-products firm developed a plan to create a world structure of subsidiaries through the acquisition of similar companies located in both developed and developing countries. Through these subsidiaries, it hoped to form a worldwide market for its products. Therefore, small- and medium-sized companies in Europe, Latin America, and Japan were purchased within a three-year period. Special efforts were made to add the U.S. products to the existing lines of the acquired companies since the consumer goods available through these foreign companies were different from those in the parent's line. However, the U.S. company ran into several problems using this strategy. Not only had it failed to consider the tastes of its potential customers, in most cases the U.S. products did not meet foreign requirements. Furthermore, the marketing, advertising, and promotional techniques which had produced such a long record of company success in the United States were not appropriate for the foreign environments. Due to the lack of supermarkets and retail chain outlets, lower standards of living, limited TV advertising exposure, and lower levels of literacy, the U.S. techniques proved ineffective in these new markets.[9]

Flaunting American ownership has also created disharmony in the foreign markets of a few companies. One U.S. firm undoubtedly regrets its wave of patriotism. Trying to revamp a newly purchased Spanish company, the U.S. manufacturer changed the original company name from a prestigious Spanish one to that of the U.S. parent. It also flew the American flag from the company flagpole and highly touted the new technology being introduced. An interview in a prominent U.S. business publication, in which the new management boasted of its effort to revitalize the Spanish operation, also angered the Spaniards who were associated with the company. They felt the U.S. company was belittling the previous Spanish management. The hurt to the Spanish pride was so great that the Spanish press attacked, the workers staged a slowdown, and the local authorities made the conduction of normal company business quite difficult.

An unfortunate decision made by Gillette nearly cost the company the razor-blade market. The firm had developed a superior stainless steel blade, but because the new blade was so outstanding and would require fewer replacements, the company was afraid to market it. So Gillette sold the technology to a British garden-tool manufacturer, Wilkinson. Because Gillette had assumed that Wilkinson would only use the new technology in the production of its garden tools, the arrangement failed to restrict Wilkinson from competing in the razor-blade market. However, Wilkinson Sword Blades were promptly introduced and sold as fast as they could be made. Gillette's superior marketing skills and experience in the razor-blade market enabled it to recover eventually, but the challenge was unwelcome and expensive.

SUMMARY

False assumptions frequently cause expensive blunders. One of the most common assumptions is that conditions that exist at home also exist abroad. Another frequently assumed idea is that what works well at home will also work well overseas. It should be abundantly clear that these are two of the most dangerous assumptions that can be made by marketing managers. Few things are the same everywhere, and almost no strategy works well everywhere.

Strategic blunders are generally not as entertaining to read about as some of the other multinational marketing mistakes, but they are usually more critical to the firm and thus more important to avoid. Although pricing errors can normally be quickly corrected, logistical problems can be very difficult to overcome. A few strategic blunders have even resulted in millions of lost dollars. There are no simple shortcuts to avoid strategic errors. The development of a marketing strategy requires care and attention. The advice of locals can be helpful, but market tests, research, and feasibility studies are also needed.

7 MARKET RESEARCH

One of the worst strategic errors a corporation can make is the failure to determine if a market exists for its products or services prior to market entry. Unfortunately, many firms have fallen prey to this mistake by blindly assuming that their products would be desirable. At times, they have been "right" (perhaps "lucky" might be more appropriate). Other times, however, they have not been so fortunate. Often the market simply was not as promising as anticipated. Several firms have discovered only after initial entry attempts that no market ever existed. Good market research would have revealed these and other avoidable problems corporations have encountered in international business.

INSUFFICIENT MARKET

Companies trying to export food products seem to have been especially prone to experiencing a great deal of difficulty in foreign markets. An American manufacturer of cornflakes, for example, tried to introduce its product to the Japanese, but the attempt failed miserably. Since the Japanese were simply not interested in the general concept of breakfast cereals, how could the manufacturer expect them to purchase cornflakes?

After learning that ketchup was not available in Japan, a U.S. company is reported to have shipped the Japanese a large quantity of its popular brand-name ketchup. Unfortunately, the firm did not stop to wonder why ketchup was not already marketed in Japan. The large, affluent Japanese market was so tempting the firm feared any delay would permit its competition to spot the "opportunity" and capture the market. A market test would have clearly revealed the reason ketchup was not sold; soy sauce was the preferred condiment. This anecdote ends more happily than many, however. The company involved was able to purchase Japanese soy sauce for profitable resale in the United States (a possible variation of the old saying "if you can't beat them, join them").

Kentucky Fried Chicken reportedly found itself in a similar situation when it attempted to enter the Brazilian market. Hoping to eventually open 100 stores, the company began operations in São Paulo. Sales, though, were unexpectedly low. Why? The firm had not thoroughly researched the possible competition. A local variety of low-priced charcoal broiled chicken was available on almost every corner of the city. Because this chicken was locally considered tastier than the Colonel's recipe, Kentucky Fried Chicken hastily revised its plans and tried to sell hamburgers, Mexican tacos, and enchiladas. The company's troubles were not over, however, for these products were practically unknown in Brazil and met with little customer interest.[1]

Unilever was forced to temporarily withdraw from one of its foreign markets when it learned the hard way that the French were not interested in its frozen foods. Happily, the company was able to later return offering products of more interest to the French.

CPC International met some resistance when it tried to sell its dry Knorr soups in the United States. The company had test marketed the product by serving passersby a small portion of its already-prepared warm soup. After the taste test, the individuals were questioned about possible sales. The research revealed U.S. interest, but sales were very low once the packages were placed on grocery-store shelves. Further investigation indicated that the market tests had overlooked the American tendency to avoid most dry soups. During the testing, those interviewed were unaware they were tasting a dried soup. Finding the taste quite acceptable, the interviewees indicated they would be willing to buy it. Had they known the soup was sold in a dry form and that during preparation it required 15-20 minutes of occasional stirring, they would have shown less interest in the product. In this particular case, the preparation was extremely important, and the failure to test for this unique difference resulted in a sluggish market.

Clever marketing-staff members often analyze product differences and try to use them to the company's advantage. Based on a research study conducted in the United States, one American firm introduced a new cake mix in England. Believing that the housewife should feel as if she is participating in the preparation of the cake mix, the U.S. marketers devised the scheme "to add an egg." Thinking they had hit upon a new consumer approach, they tried to sell the mix in England. The mix proved to be a failure, though, because the Britons do not like fancy American cakes. They prefer cakes that are tough and spongy and can accompany afternoon tea. Simply adding an egg just did not eliminate the basic style and taste differences.

Numerous other companies have also experienced difficulties when trying to market products that have specific tastes. Tastes desirable to some are often unacceptable to others. Occasionally, a flavor can be successfully modified, but many times it is just totally inappropriate. Warner encountered this when it tried to sell a cinnamon-flavored "Freshen-up" gum in Chile. Because the gum's taste was unacceptable there, it fared poorly in the marketplace. Coca-Cola also tried to market a product in Chile with little success. When the company attempted to introduce a new grape-flavored drink, it discovered that the Chileans were not interested. Apparently, the grape flavor is unacceptable; wine is the preferred grape drink.

Chase and Sanborn met resistance when it tried to introduce its instant coffee in France. In the French home, the consumption of coffee plays more of a ceremonial role than in the English home. The preparation of "real" coffee is a touchstone in the life of the French housewife, so she will generally reject instant coffee because its casual characteristics do not fit into the French pattern.

A poorly located sales outlet can also contribute to an insufficient market. As was mentioned in the first chapter, one hamburger chain experienced low sales levels when it located a franchise close to a bordello. Another company, McDonald's, chose an inappropriate location when it first expanded to Europe. The company opened an outlet in a suburb of Amsterdam but soon learned that to attract adequate local traffic, the store should have been placed downtown. Once the company moved into town, sales immediately improved.

Of course, food companies are not the only firms that have had trouble selling products in foreign markets. The Cummins Engine Company of Indiana tried to introduce its diesel engines in Europe, but sales were sluggish because the major European truck manufacturers also produced their own engines. Cummins was not accustomed to this local integrated system. Although Cummins denies the report that it had been unaware of the extensive integration before it entered the market, the company does concede that the market was more competitive than expected.

Consumers' lifestyles vary, and firms must consider these differences when attempting market entry. Just as sales can suffer due to poor store locations or unexpected competition, sales can also be hurt through inappropriate product applications. One company became aware of this when it tried to market aerosol-spray furniture polish in one of the less-developed countries. Analysis of the local average income levels suggested that the natives could afford the product. This type of data, though, is often misleading; in many countries, most of the wealth is concentrated and owned by a few. Therefore, average income levels erroneously indicate that many people in a population can afford a product. In this case, only the few individuals who enjoyed the high incomes could afford the "luxury" of an aerosol-spray furniture polish. Even they, however, were not interested in the product; such labor-saving devices were not felt to be necessary for their servants.

Sometimes the relevant factor determining a product's success involves the technological advancement of the potential customer. A sophisticated product may elicit interest during market testing but may fail in the marketplace because it receives a predictably erroneous reputation of being undependable. Corporations have discovered this fact all too frequently. For example, one company manufactured a product far superior to any being used in a particular African nation. Since market tests indicated strong consumer interest, the firm introduced the product. Shortly thereafter, word spread that the product was not reliable. This was not true, however. The product broke because the new owners did not understand its maintenance requirements. They refused to oil it even though they were instructed to do so. Because this maintenance was atypical of their lifestyle, they soon returned to their earlier, more primitive tools which required no special care. In effect, no market existed for these advanced products.

In some cases, it becomes necessary for a firm to develop a totally new product, one that is completely stripped of frills or complex features. This process, involving the development of simpler products, is often referred to as "reverse engineering" or "inventing backward." General Motors successfully used this process during the development of its Basic Transportation Vehicle. Singer has profited from its introduction of a basic hand-powered sewing machine.

Although the United States consists of 50 states, the country is usually considered one market. Naturally, subtle cultural differences exist among the states. Neighboring districts in other parts of the world, however, often represent vastly different cultures even though they may be as geographically close as neighboring states. This close proximity to vastly different cultures is hard for many American managers to fully understand. The Sunbeam company, for example, assumed that since West Germans consumed substantial amounts of toast, the Italians would also. To the company's misfortune, it soon discovered that this did not prove to be the case. The firm encountered additional problems in Italy when it tried to introduce the ladies electric shaver. Although sales had been fairly strong in some parts of Europe, they remained poor in Italy. Apparently Italian men prefer women with unshaved legs.

People speaking similar languages do not necessarily represent totally similar cultures, either. One American company, assuming that a similar language must indicate similar tastes, tried to sell a U.S. after-shave lotion in England. An expensive advertising campaign was launched but failed. Why? The average British male saw no functional value in the use of after-shave lotion. In fact, the British men even felt that the use of scents was effeminate.

Governments have also been known to initiate projects and only later realize that no one really wanted what they had to offer. At the end of World War II, the U.S. government shipped a load of corn to Bulgaria to feed the starving people. However, because the Bulgarians considered corn to be lowly food fit only for hogs, they never touched it. This incident even sparked the Communist party to disseminate propaganda expounding that the capitalistic United States had sent pig's food to needy people.

Numerous governments have tried to send aid to some of the developing countries. Sometimes, however, even well-intended gifts have been almost useless. At one time, for example, great quantities of milk powder were distributed in South America. Claiming that the milk made them ill, the natives reluctantly used it instead to whitewash their houses. Research, conducted to determine exactly what was happening, revealed that the natives were correct. It was discovered that an enzyme necessary for the breakdown of milk is retained by North Americans and Europeans throughout their lives. Many South Americans, on the other hand, retain the enzyme only while of nursing age. Therefore, the older children and adults were unable to digest the milk. No demand for this product existed even though it was free!

INADEQUATE FEASIBILITY STUDIES

It should now be obvious that a firm needs to conduct market research to help determine the existence of an adequate market. This research must be performed carefully since an inadequate feasibility study may prove more disastrous for the company than none at all.

For instance, one company that chose to cut costs and save time opted to use a feasibility study that a competitor had conducted earlier. At the time the study was originally undertaken, the investment was regarded favorably by the Asian government and the opportunity seemed encouraging. However, local conditions changed during the time that had elapsed. As a result, the firm built its plant but immediately experienced difficulties. The company's use of an outdated feasibility study caused it to overestimate the positive results and underestimate the probable problems.

Many firms have created headaches for themselves by acting before sufficient data had been gathered. Consider, for example, a well-known U.S. manufacturer of nondurable consumer goods that formed a partnership with a local Japanese company. The Japanese firm supplied encouraging data so, after a one-week investigation by the assistant to the president, the U.S. manufacturer quickly agreed to the arrangement. Not too surprisingly, the venture fell short of expectations. Even with a complete change of top management, the investment stagnated. The company's hasty entry decision had been based upon an inadequate market analysis and the belief that the market would welcome the entry of prestigious U.S. brands. The firm had assumed that it could easily win the confidence of the marketplace and take over a sizable percentage of it. Had the company conducted a thorough feasibility study and developed a plan for start-up operations, it would have discovered that the Japanese were not necessarily an homogeneous people in terms of social and economic characteristics and that the firm had mistakenly assumed that local marketing lacked sophistication. This knowledge could have enhanced the planners' abilities to develop a more prosperous venture.[2]

After a market research team indicated the existence of an adequate market, one Swiss pharmaceutical firm built an $8 million manufacturing plant in Southeast Asia. The researchers, though, had overlooked an extremely important aspect of the market— the local black market controlled by government officials. Because of this added competition, the firm experienced lower earnings than expected and found itself with excess production capacity.

Sometimes what appears to be a thorough feasibility study simply is not. After conducting what was believed to be an intensive study, one firm discovered that a number of factors that should have been considered prior to its entrance abroad had been overlooked. Initial research confirmed the desirability of erecting an iron and steel mill, but the mill was forced to close its doors within one year. All equipment was removed and the building was stripped. Those involved in the feasibility study had correctly surmised the availability of labor. They had failed, however, to indicate that the country under consideration was one in which private ownership was inconsistent with the policies of social reform prevalent within the government. Almost all manufacturing was publicly owned and operated. The laborers, many of whom had been exploited on the farms which most had left, were encouraged to believe in "capitalistic exploitation." Consequently, they constantly demanded higher wages and increased benefits. Labor unrest, low output, and poor quality resulted. The feasibility study should have revealed this popular "public ownership" ideology. Since another firm had failed earlier in a similar investment for similar reasons, the investors should have been tipped off that a recurrence of the problem was likely.[3]

As a final example, consider the experience of the Rheem company in the Italian market. The firm's initial strategy of buying raw materials from a local firm, ISI, also included plans to sell the finished product, welded pipes, locally. The plan was put into operation, but Rheem soon learned that not only did ISI produce the same welded pipe, it also maintained good, inside contacts with the major buyer of the pipe—the government. Because Rheem was buying its raw material from ISI, it was unable to undercut ISI's price and, as a foreign-owned firm, it was not able to get the Italian government contracts. Unfortunately, it had not developed export plans either. Thorough research should have uncovered these problems and would have encouraged Rheem to consider alternative plans.

As evidenced, a firm's reliance on outdated or incomplete feasibility studies can cause it to blunder. Improperly conducted studies can also create difficulties. This is easily illustrated by a classic story which involves the market research conducted some years ago by *Reader's Digest*. The researchers concluded from their findings that more spaghetti was consumed by West Germans and French than by Italians. Further analysis revealed that this false finding surfaced as a result of the questions asked. The survey questions dealt with the purchases of branded and packaged spaghetti. Many Italians, however, buy spaghetti in bulk. By qualifying the way in which the product was purchased, the researchers arrived at the false conclusion about the amounts of spaghetti consumed. To conduct good market research, one must pay strict attention to both method and content.[4]

THE ROLE OF MARKET RESEARCH

Not only could proper market research have aided companies in avoiding the problems reported in this chapter, it could have served to reduce or eliminate many of the blunders discussed throughout the entire book. Market researchers have the ability to uncover adaptation needs, potential name problems, promotional requirements, and proper market strategies. Even many of the translation blunders could have been avoided if good research techniques had been employed.

A number of the cited blunders occurred because firms tried to use the same product, name, promotional material, or strategy overseas as they used at home. They were simply hoping that what worked well at home would also work well abroad. Although often an unrealistic hope, this is nevertheless understandable. Corporations must minimize costs, and standardization usually permits cost reduction.

Even though standardization promotes certain efficiencies, in many instances it is not a worthwhile strategy to pursue. Limitations do exist, and it is important for firms to recognize and understand them. Various barriers to standardized international markets are cited in Table 7-1.

TABLE 7-1
Some barriers to standardized international marketing

Obstacles to uniformity	Marketing ingredients			
	Product	Price	Distribution	Promotion
Economic factors	Varied income levels	Varied income levels	Different retail structures	Media availability
Cultural factors	Consumer tastes and habits	Price negotiating habit	Shopping habits	Language, attitude differences
Competitive factors	Nature of existing products	Competitors' costs and prices	Competitors' monopoly of channels	Competitors' budgets, appeals
Legal factors	Product regulations	Price controls	Restrictions on distribution	Advertising and media restrictions

Source: From Vern Terpstra, *International Dimensions of Marketing* (Boston: Kent Publishing Company, 1981), p. 10. © 1981 by Wadsworth, Inc. Reprinted by permission of Kent Publishing, a Division of Wadsworth, Inc., 20 Providence Street, Boston, MA 02116.

The use of market research enables a firm to determine its limits of standardization. But in its broadest sense, market research serves two major functions: It can help a company identify what can be accomplished and it can help a firm realize what should and should not be done.

Few would question the value of market research as part of international business planning. Unfortunately, it is not an easy undertaking and is extremely complex. Even the smallest of details must not be ignored during analysis. Therefore, the list of research variables is quite lengthy. In fact, Business International identifies 70 factors that should be investigated during the collection of information regarding a foreign market. These items have been classified into the following categories: import regulations, port and transportation facilities, distribution patterns, credit, advertising, legal, and statistics.[5] Business International also provides a list of 41 factors that should be screened prior to the introduction of a new product. These have been grouped as organization factors, searching ideas, screening factors, market considerations, distribution considerations, packagings, and other considerations.[6]

The well-known Farmer-Richman model for analyzing foreign environments stresses 29 variables. These are grouped under four major headings: educational characteristics, sociological characteristics, political-legal characteristics, and economic characteristics.[7]

In his textbook on international marketing, Warren Keegan identifies 25 categories of a global business intelligence system. Listed under "Market Information" are: market potential, consumer/customer attitudes and behavior, channels of distribution, communication media, market sources, new products, competitive sales, competitive marketing programs and plans, competitive products, competitive operations, and competitive investments. Under "Prescriptive Information," Dr. Keegan reports foreign exchanges, foreign taxes, other foreign laws, and U.S. laws. Manpower, money, raw material and acquisition-merger data are included under "Resource Information." Additionally, cited under "General Conditions" are economic factors, social factors, political factors, scientific/technological factors, management and administrative practices, and other information.[8]

Philip Cateora and John Hess, in their international marketing textbook, mention 14 "foreign factors" which require research. Variables included are: competition, transportation, electrical characteristics, trade barriers, economic environment, business philosophies, legal systems, social customs, languages, political climate, consumption patterns, relevant cultural patterns, religious and moral backgrounds, and philosophies of major political parties.[9]

One of the more difficult and important challenges of international marketing research is the cross-cultural analysis of consumer behavior. Six key tasks have been identified: (1) determination of relevant motivations of the culture, (2) determination of characteristic behavior patterns, (3) determination of what broad cultural values are relevant to the product, (4) determination of characteristic forms of decision making, (5) evaluation of promotional methods appropriate to the culture, and (6) determination of appropriate institutions for the product in the minds of the consumer.[10]

All of these lists indicate that the area of international marketing research has drawn a great deal of attention. Various experts hold differing opinions about which specific variables should be studied, but general agreement exists about the value of collecting and analyzing data. Specific data requirements depend upon the firm, its products, and the decision being made. Different sets of data are needed if a company is determining whether or not to go abroad, which countries to enter, how to enter the foreign markets, or what the best marketing strategies are. Research methodology must be appropriate for the particular situation. There is no short, simple list of variables all firms should always consider.

SUMMARY

This chapter has focused on the importance of determining potential market existence, the necessity of feasibility studies, and the role of market research. On numerous occasions, companies as well as governments have blundered either because no market studies were initiated or the ones conducted were inadequate.

The importance of international marketing research has been stressed throughout this book. Because numerous texts have been written specifically dealing with international marketing research,[11] this book does not attempt to duplicate those endeavors. It does, however, cite numerous examples of company errors which could have been avoided through the use of proper research techniques.

EPILOGUE

This collection of international business blunders was not gathered with the intention of using it to poke fun at multinational corporations or to make them appear inept. Rather, it was assembled to provide valuable, vicarious examples of business practices that should be avoided. The blunders others have made provide us with interesting lessons that are surely preferable to learning through experience.

In reality, companies are generally quite competent. Considering the many ways a firm can blunder, it must be doing most things correctly just to survive. This thought was best expressed by a senior executive from General Motors when he was asked to verify one of the problems reported in this book. He replied that although GM may have made a few errors overseas, when that very small number is compared to the many decisions made by GM, it is "a good batting average." This is true. Most firms make few serious mistakes and even fewer avoidable blunders. If they did, they simply would not be in business long. Although numerous errors have been committed, one must realize that the mistakes are spread throughout a number of companies over a number of years.

The fact that firms make these mistakes should not be all that surprising anyway. After all, it is not really a company that blunders, but its employees. Employees are only human, and we all make mistakes. Sometimes the errors are personal, but sometimes they are made on behalf of corporations.

It should also be noted that the blunders reported may not be totally accurate. Although most of the anecdotes have been reported in the media and efforts were made to verify them, verification has not been easy. Many corporations have been reluctant to respond to inquiries. Several firms have replied with something like "we are sorry but we cannot provide you with the information about that possible event. The person who had been responsible for that area is *no longer with the company.*" These statements possibly bear an added message: If one wants to remain with a firm, avoid making blunders.

Since firms do not appreciate appearing foolish, they sometimes deny a witnessed event. But as the public becomes more and more aware that all firms have made some mistakes, corporate denials become less necessary. There are cases, however, where reports of company blunders have proven to be false. The wrong companies have been identified or the entire story has been fictionalized. This author discovered an excellent example of a false report when trying to verify a story regarding Exxon's ventures in Thailand. The report stated that Exxon's ad, "Put a tiger in your tank" failed in Thailand because the tiger does not represent power and strength there. However, a series of letters and investigations in both Asia and the United States revealed what had really happened. Over-zealous competitors had deliberately planted the false story for the U.S. media to pick up. In fact, not only is the tiger a symbol of strength in Thailand, Exxon continued to use the ad effectively and was able to capture a larger share of the local market.

Unfortunately, this book may also contain a few errors. Naturally, any error is greatly regretted. There certainly have also been errors of omission because the book does not cite or report every blunder ever committed.

One final word of warning: No one should be under the illusion that all blunders have been made; others are likely to occur. The more we learn of these blunders, the more we will understand them and their causes and the better we can prepare ourselves to avoid future blunders. Hopefully, this book will help reduce the number of blunders made. We do not want your future decisions to end up being reported in the next edition of this book.

NOTES

Chapter 1

1. An excellent discussion of this widely reported error appeared in *The Wall Street Journal,* February 20, 1969, p. 2. Note that the $55 million loss was in 1969 dollars!

2. The pineapple blunder was initially reported by John S. Ewing in "The Lessons to be Learned—American Industry in Developing Countries," *Columbia Journal of World Business,* November-December 1969, pp. 83-84. It should be noted that others have subsequently cited Del Monte as the company involved, but this is not the case. Another firm was the unfortunate one.

3. Vern Terpstra, *International Dimensions of Marketing* (Boston: Kent Publishing, 1982), p. 44.

4. More information on this and similar incidents is reported by Edward T. Hall in *The Silent Language* (New York: Doubleday, 1959).

5. A 32-page booklet, *International Business Gift-Giving Customs* by Kathleen Reardon, deals with the problems of international gift-giving. It is available through the Parker Pen Company, P.O. Box 5100, Janesville, Wisconsin 53547 ($5 a copy).

6. Edward T. Hall, "The Silent Language in Overseas Business," *Harvard Business Review,* May-June 1960, pp. 87-96.

7. Melville J. Herskovits, *Man and His Work* (New York: Alfred A. Knopf, 1952), p. 634.

8. Richard N. Farmer and Barry M. Richman, *International Business,* 3d ed. (Bloomington, Ind.: Cedarwood Press, 1980), pp. 80-83.

9. *The Cultural Environment of International Business* by Vern Terpstra (South-Western Publishing, 1978) is highly recommended for those interested in a much more thorough discussion of the role culture plays in international business.

10. Although no agreement exists on exactly what constitutes nonverbal forms of communication, there are several interesting publications on the subject. Three of the most helpful are: Michael Argyle, *Social Interaction* (New York: Atherton, 1969); Edward T. Hall, *The Silent Language* (New York: Doubleday, 1959); and Dale G. Leathers, *Nonverbal Communication Systems* (Boston: Allyn & Bacon, 1976). Two other publications of interest include: S. O. Duncan, "Nonverbal Communication," *Psychological Bulletin* 72, no. 2 (1969), pp. 118-37; and A. E. Scheflen, *Body Language and the Social Order* (Englewood Cliffs, N.J.: Prentice-Hall, 1972).

Chapter 2

1. More information regarding the troubles encountered by the Campbell Soup Company is reported in "The $30 Million Lesson," *Sales Management,* March 1, 1967, pp. 31-. Although the problems concerning the soup can size are possibly the most widely known, the company also experienced a variety of adaptation and marketing difficulties.

2. For more information about the Jell-O experience, read "Managers away from Home," *Fortune,* August 15, 1969, pp. 56-.

3. A more complete discussion of this point can be found in James A. Lee, "Cultural Analysis in Overseas Operations," *Harvard Business Review,* March-April 1966, pp. 106-14.

4. The latest available report regarding this problem is "GM Runs into a Middle East Crisis: It's Too Hot and Dusty in

Baghdad," *The Wall Street Journal,* February 23, 1982, p. 37. The article contains more data but does not describe the final outcome.

5. Many versions of this historical event exist. Most historians, however, currently seem to believe that the bullets encased in pig wax represented the "final straw." Basically, the bullets provided an example of the degree of British insensitivity to Indian cultural values and needs. In reality, the East India Company needed to modify its entire operation.

6. See Albert Stridsberg, "U.S. Advertisers Win Some, Lose Some, in Foreign Market," *Advertising Age,* May 6, 1974, p. 18, for additional information about U.S. corporate experiences with soups in overseas countries.

7. For a full report on the Ford problem in Europe, read Gregory H. Wierzynski, "The Battle for the European Auto Market," *Fortune,* September 15, 1968, pp. 119-.

8. The complaint voiced by Colgate-Palmolive dealt with the possibility of consumers mistaking the two products. Although many firms face competition from counterfeit products, Unilever argued that it was not attempting any such strategy. However, Australian courts ruled that the resemblance was too great. For details, read Len Blanket, "Aussi Court Bans Package Ad," *Advertising Age,* October 12, 1981, p. 72.

Chapter 3

1. By reporting this incident in some of its annual reports, Coca-Cola has even laughed at itself.

2. It should be noted, however, that reports citing problems with the name "Cue" have been denied by the company.

3. For a more complete discussion of this problem, see Robert D. Buzzell, "Can You Standardize Multinational Marketing?" *Harvard Business Review,* November-December 1968, pp. 102-13.

4. Although the October 1, 1963, issue of *Forbes* reported

this case in the article "General Mills: the General and Betty Crocker," pp. 20-24, General Mills now denies the report.

5. For further details, see Carolyn Pfaff, "Champagne Cigs Cause Headache," *Advertising Age,* March 30, 1981, p. 2.

6. Background information is provided by Pat Sloan in "Fragrance under Fire: Opium Ads Go Up in Smoke," *Advertising Age,* June 4, 1979, p. 1.

Chapter 4

1. For more details, see M. Y. Yoshino, "So You're Setting up Shop in Asia," *Columbia Journal of World Business,* November-December 1967, pp. 61-66.

2. A more complete account of these two "awards" can be found in "Canadian Sexist Ads Got Rapped," *Advertising Age,* July 6, 1981, p. 28.

3. American firms have generally encountered great difficulties trying to sell to the Japanese. An early article that discusses some of the problems and how to deal with them is "How to Get Madison Avenue 'Sell' into Japanese Ad Campaigns," *Business Abroad,* October 30, 1967, pp. 26-29.

4. This incident and several other business problems are reported by Stephen Winkworth in *Great Commercial Disasters* (London: Macmillan London Ltd., 1980).

5. Business International Corporation, *151 Checklists* (New York, 1974), pp. 145-46.

6. Philip R. Cateora and John M. Hess, *International Marketing,* 4th ed. (Homewood, Ill.: Richard D. Irwin, 1979), p. 417.

7. An early discussion regarding this was presented by Raphael W. Hodgson and Hugo E. R. Uyterhoeven in "Analyzing Foreign Opportunities," *Harvard Business Review,* March-April 1962, pp. 60-79.

8. This problem was first reported by Charles Winick in "Anthropology's Contribution to Marketing," *Journal of Marketing,* July 1961, pp. 53-60.

9. Cateora and Hess, *International Marketing*, pp. 109-10.

10. For additional information regarding the challenges and problems involved in reaching the Hispanic community in the United States, see "How Ads Were Changed to Reach Minorities," *Advertising Age*, April 7, 1980, pp. 5-23.

11. It should be pointed out, however, that at last report all avenues of appeal had not been exhausted. As multinational managers know, it is not easy to win a case against foreign firms in foreign courts.

Chapter 5

1. Although many people have cited the "pregnancy" problem experienced by Parker Pen, they seldom provide any details. The author, therefore, thanks the Parker Pen Company management for its open and refreshingly frank discussion of this past event and what caused it. All firms have at one time or another made mistakes. If more firms would be as helpful as the Parker Pen Company, then we could all more clearly understand the underlying causes of these errors and avoid them in the future.

2. This translation problem has been frequently cited essentially because an entire article was based upon the minor incident. Edward M. Mazze wrote "How to Push a Body Abroad without Making It a Corpse," *Business Abroad*, August 10, 1964, p. 15, and more than a dozen others have mentioned it since. All of this talk surrounding the incident has been far more unpleasant for GM than the actual event.

3. For a brief discussion about international business blunders, see John Train, "Costly Imbroglios," *Forbes*, July 20, 1981, pp. 120-21.

4. It should be noted that the company denies it experienced these translation difficulties in Germany but does admit the ad was misunderstood in Asia. Indeed, the phrase "Come Alive with Pepsi" must have created a real challenge for translators in many parts of the world. If the company encountered problems in only one or two countries, it should consider itself quite fortunate.

5. This list was adapted from Maurice Brisebois, "Industrial Advertising and Marketing in Quebec," *The Marketer*, Spring-Summer 1966, p. 10.

6. "Translating Can Be Beastly," *Spectrum Newsletter*, Spring 1981, p. 2.

Chapter 6

1. For more information about this widely reported blunder, see Stephen Winkworth, *Great Commercial Disasters* (London: Macmillan London Ltd., 1980), p. 56.

2. A more complete account is provided by Simon Williams in "Negotiating Investment in Emerging Countries," *Harvard Business Review*, January-February 1965, pp. 89-99.

3. Additional information is reported in "Simmons in Japan—No Bed of Roses," *Sales Management*, August 1, 1967, pp. 27-.

4. A more complete discussion of this complex development is provided by Douglas F. Lamont in *Managing Foreign Investment in Southern Italy* (New York: Praeger Publishers, 1978), pp. 114-15.

5. An interesting account of the Imperial-Eastman experience is reported in "What We Did Right and Some Boners We Pulled," *Business Abroad*, February 5, 1968, pp. 19-20.

6. For more information, read W. D. Dance, "An Evolving Structure for Multinational Operations," *Columbia Journal of World Business*, November-December 1969, pp. 25-30.

7. "Golden Touches Turned to Lead," *Time*, November 30, 1981, p. 66.

8. Massey Ferguson claims that the problems were not predictable and were primarily caused by the Turkish government. Outside reports, however, lay more of the blame on management. See, for example, "Turkey Cancels Plans for Tractor Output by Massey Ferguson," *The Wall Street Journal*, November 18, 1970, p. 27.

9. For more information, see Myles L. Mace, "The President and International Operations," *Harvard Business Review,* November-December 1966, pp. 72-84.

Chapter 7

1. Jose Penteado, Jr., "U.S. Fast Foods Move Slowly," *Advertising Age,* May 25, 1981, pp. 5-8.

2. This widely cited example and conclusion were first reported by M. Y. Yoshino in "So You're Setting up Shop in Asia," *Columbia Journal of World Business,* November-December 1967, pp. 61-66.

3. For additional information, see Simon Williams, "Negotiating Investment in Emerging Countries," *Harvard Business Review,* January-February 1965, pp. 89-99.

4. A more complete discussion of this is provided by Philip R. Cateora and John M. Hess in *International Marketing,* 4th ed. (Homewood, Ill.: Richard D. Irwin, 1979), p. 271.

5. Business International, *151 Checklists* (New York, 1974), pp. 83-84.

6. Ibid., pp. 89-90.

7. Richard N. Farmer and Barry M. Richman, *International Business,* 3d ed. (Bloomington, Ind.: Cedarwood Press, 1980), pp. 80-83.

8. Warren Keegan, *Multinational Marketing Management,* 2d ed. (Englewood Cliffs, N.J.: Prentice-Hall, 1980), pp. 186-87.

9. Cateora and Hess, *International Marketing,* p. 255.

10. James F. Engel, David T. Kollat, and Roger D. Blackwell, *Consumer Behavior,* 2d ed. (New York: Holt, Rinehart & Winston, 1973), pp. 95-96.

11. See the Bibliography for a partial listing.

BIBLIOGRAPHY

— Aman, Reinhold. "New, Improved Dreck! Interlingual Taboo in Personal Names, Brand Names, and Language Learning." *Maledicta,* Winter 1979, pp. 145-52.

Armao, Rosemary. "Worst Blunders: Firms Laugh through Tears." *American Business,* January 1981, p. 12.

Arpan, J. S.; D. A. Ricks; and D. J. Patton. "The Meaning of Miscues Made by Multinationals." *Management International Review,* 1974, 4-5, pp. 3-16.

Baker, James C., and John K. Ryans, Jr. *Multinational Marketing: Dimensions in Strategy.* Columbus, Ohio: Grid, 1975.

› Ball, Donald A., and Wendell H. MuCulloch, Jr. *International Business: Introduction and Essentials.* Plano, Tex.: Business Publications, 1982.

Black, Gilbert J. "Tighten Your Overseas Marketing Plan." *Sales Marketing Today,* August-September 1969.

Bowen, F. A. "Ad Bloopers Abroad—Amusing and Sometimes Costly." *F. A. Bowen Reports,* Janesville, Wis.

Business International. *151 Checklists.* New York: Business International Corporation, 1974.

Buzzell, Robert D. "Can You Standardize Multinational Marketing?" *Harvard Business Review,* November-December 1968, pp. 102-13.

Cateora, Philip R. *International Marketing.* 5th ed. Homewood, Ill.: Richard D. Irwin, 1983.

"Corporate-Size Blunders Provide Laughs and Lessons." *Chicago Tribune,* December 28, 1980, Section 5, p. 6.

Daniels, John D.; Ernest W. Ogram, Jr.; and Lee H. Radebaugh. *International Business: Environments and Operations.* 2d ed. Reading, Mass.: Addison-Wesley, 1979.

Engel, James F.; David T. Kollat; and Roger D. Blackwell. *Consumer Behavior.* 2d ed. New York: Holt, Rinehart & Winston, 1973.

Farmer, Richard N., and Barry M. Richman. *International Business.* 3d ed. Bloomington, Ind.: Cedarwood Press, 1980.

Fayerweather, John. *International Business Strategy and Administration.* Cambridge, Mass.: Ballinger Publishing, 1978.

Halborg, Al. "How to Use Names." *Management Today,* November 1979, pp. 113-16.

Hall, Edward T. *Beyond Culture.* Garden City, N.Y.: Anchor Press/Doubleday, 1976.

_____. *The Silent Language.* New York: Doubleday, 1959.

_____. "The Silent Language in Overseas Business." *Harvard Business Review,* May-June 1960, pp. 87-96.

Hill, G. Christian. "More Firms Turn to Translation Experts to Avoid Costly, Embarrassing Mistakes." *The Wall Street Journal,* January 13, 1977, p. 34.

"How Ads Were Changed to Reach Minorities." *Advertising Age,* April 7, 1980, pp. 5-.

"Interpreter de Rigueur for Marketing Abroad." *American Business,* November 1979, p. 23.

Kahler, Ruel, and Roland L. Kramer. *International Marketing.* 4th ed. Cincinnati: South-Western Publishing, 1977.

Keegan, Warren J. *Multinational Marketing Management.* 2d ed. Englewood Cliffs, N.J.: Prentice-Hall, 1980.

Kolde, Endel J. *Environment of International Business.* Boston: Kent Publishing, 1982.

League, Frederick A. "Why Companies Fail Abroad." *Columbia Journal of World Business,* July-August 1968, pp. 55-.

Lee, James A. "Cultural Analysis in Overseas Operations." *Harvard Business Review,* March-April 1966, pp. 106-14.

Mace, Myles L. "The President and International Operations." *Harvard Business Review,* November-December 1966, pp. 72-84.

Manville, Richard. "33 Caveats for the Prospective Overseas Marketer." *Marketing News,* March 10, 1978, pp. 6-7.

Mauser, Ferdinand F. "Losing Something in Translation." *Harvard Business Review,* July-August 1977, pp. 5-6.

Mayer, Charles S. "The Lessons of Multinational Marketing Research." *Business Horizons,* November-December 1978, pp. 7-13.

Phatak, Arvind V. *International Dimensions of Management.* Boston: Kent Publishing, 1982.

Reardon, Kathleen. *International Business Gift-Giving Customs: A Guide for American Executives.* Janesville, Wis.: The Parker Pen Company, 1981.

Ricks, David A.; Jeffrey S. Arpan; and Marilyn Y. C. Fu. "Pitfalls in Advertising Overseas." *Journal of Advertising Research,* December 1974, pp. 47-51.

Ricks, David A.; Marilyn Y. C. Fu; and Jeffrey S. Arpan. *International Business Blunders.* Columbus, Ohio: Grid, 1974.

Robinson, Richard D. *International Business Management: A Guide to Decision Making.* 2d ed. Hinsdale, Ill.: Dryden Press, 1978.

Robock, Stefan H.; Kenneth Simmonds; and Jack Zwick. *International Business and Multinational Enterprises.* 2d ed. Homewood, Ill.: Richard D. Irwin, 1977.

Rotbart, Dean. "To Make Mr. Ricks' List, a Company Must Commit a Major Blunder Abroad." *The Wall Street Journal,* March 13, 1981, p. 21.

Stridsberg, Albert. "U.S. Advertisers Win Some, Lose Some in Foreign Market." *Advertising Age,* May 6, 1974, pp. 18-.

Terpstra, Vern. *International Dimensions of Marketing.* Boston: Kent Publishing, 1982.

_____. *International Marketing.* 2d ed. Hinsdale, Ill.: Dryden Press, 1978.

_____. *The Cultural Environment of International Business.* Cincinnati: South-Western Publishing, 1978.

Tharp, David. "U.S. Marketing 'No Go' in Japan." *Advertising Age,* December 11, 1978, p. 164.

"The Spanish-American Business Wars." *Worldwide P&I Planning,* May-June 1971, pp. 30-40.

Train, John. "Costly Imbroglios." *Forbes,* July 20, 1981, pp. 120-21.

Vernon, Raymond, and Louis T. Wells. *Economic Environment of International Business.* 3d ed. Englewood Cliffs, N.J.: Prentice-Hall, 1981.

_____. *Manager in the International Economy.* 4th ed. Englewood Cliffs, N.J.: Prentice-Hall, 1981.

Winick, Charles. "Anthropology's Contributions to Marketing." *Journal of Marketing,* July 1961, pp. 53-60.

Winkworth, Stephen. *Great Commercial Disasters.* London: Macmillan London Limited, 1980.

Yoshino, Michael Y. "So You're Setting Up Shop in Asia." *Columbia Journal of World Business,* November-December 1967, pp. 61-66.